1988

SCHOOL

ERNST WENK AND NORA HARLOW
EDITORS

RESPONSIBLE ACTION · DAVIS · CALIFORNIA

The cover designs for all DIALOGUE
BOOKS are created by the well known
Swiss artist Celestino Piatti

Library of Congress Card Number 78-51102
ISBN 0-931364-04-3

PREFACE

The present anthology, sponsored by the National Institute of Education and compiled by Responsible Action of Davis, California, is part of the national effort to respond to the school crime problem by gathering and disseminating information on its probable causes and potential solutions. The focus of this collection differs somewhat from that of earlier works. Causal theories and statistical data are considered important, but the primary emphasis in this collection is on *practical* approaches to school crime prevention and control. Some of the papers included in this volume were solicited for a collection of papers sponsored by the office of the Secretary of the Department of Health, Education and Welfare and compiled by the Research Center of the National Council on Crime and Delinquency. This earlier work was based on a nationwide solicitation effort to obtain an interdisciplinary collection of theoretical papers on the causes of crime in the nation's schools, with an emphasis on its relationship to poverty. The remainder of the papers were developed specifically for the present anthology. All of the submissions were condensed, some of them quite significantly. In most cases, the original full-length papers can be obtained from their respective authors.

The collection begins with two papers describing approaches to the study of crime in schools — a prerequisite to the design and implementation of effective prevention programs. Garrett, Bass, and Casserly outline a strategy for basing prevention programs on the findings of research tailored to a particular school. A model of the social organization of the high school, presented by Ianni, offers a conceptual framework for studying school crime and taking appropriate actions to prevent it.

These papers are followed by a group of seven articles which are primarily explanatory, suggesting coherent theories of causation, but which also offer concrete suggestions for altering conditions in school or society which contribute to school crime. Gold suggests that delinquent behavior in school is generated by negative school experiences and resulting low self-esteem. He identifies the characteristics of an alternative school program designed to provide students with positive experiences and reports on research in this area. Allen and Greenberger present some intriguing study findings on the aesthetics of vandalism — the factors which make destruction enjoyable — and suggest changes in design, construction, and school response which may reduce incentives for student vandalism. The lack of meaningful roles for youth in contemporary society is pinpointed by Hruska as a major cause of student disruption. He proposes a number of imaginative ways in which young people might be diverted to activities which both meet their developmental needs and benefit the community. David and Lincoln differentiate the various sources of social power, suggesting that students attack the school because they cannot deal effectively with the real source of the problem — the place of young people in society. Feldman analyzes the effects of labeling on students, while Scherer lists ways in which school-community linkages can be increased to improve the socialization process. A synthesis of two major delinquency theories, structural theory and control theory, is offered by Cernkovich and Denisoff, who also note some of its practical implications for strengthening a student's "stake in conformity."

The third category of papers differs from the second primarily in emphasis. While drawing on various theories of crime causation, these eight papers concentrate on specific programs or actions which can be taken to reduce school crime. In the first selection, Oden and MacDonald, arguing that racial discrimination in schools leads to students' alienation and crime, propose a Human Relations Training program aimed at heightening awareness of racial biases in teacher/student relationships and in school policies. Pink and Kapel suggest a model for school governance which de-politicizes the selection of school board members and more widely disperses educational decision-making throughout the community. Garbarino makes a strong case for smaller schools, pointing out that the trend toward large schools has resulted in reduced opportunities for student participation and a social climate which permits perpetrator-victim relationships to be created and to persist. De Cecco and

Roberts describe a technique for negotiating school conflicts to short-circuit the tendency toward delinquent behavior. An approach to the training of specialists to work with disruptive students is set forth by Bell and Semmel, while Duggan and Shlien report on a cross-age child care program which has been successful in redirecting the energies of troublesome adolescents. Wenk presents a new concept of community education designed to expand community involvement in the public schools and reduce alienation. Scharf's paper completes this collection with a discussion of moral education as a delinquency prevention strategy.

This work was carried out under contract NIE-P-77-0193. The views expressed in the various papers are the authors' and do not necessarily represent those of the federal government or the National Institute of Education. Publication of this anthology was made possible through a collaborative effort of the National Institute of Education, the Office of the Secretary of the Department of Health, Education and Welfare, the National Council on Crime and Delinquency, and Responsible Action, Inc. Support of the staff of these various agencies and organizations is thankfully acknowledged. Of particular assistance to this project were Dr. Keith Baker of the Office of the Assistant Secretary for Planning and Evaluation of HEW and Dr. Oliver Moles of the National Institute of Education. The contributions of Suzanne Mikesell (copy-editing), Gwen Dodsley (typing) and Carrie Honeycutt (typesetting) also are acknowledged.

It is hoped that this varied selection of papers will contribute to a fuller understanding of the school crime problem. An even more important objective of this volume, however, is to aid school personnel in developing effective responses to crime in their schools, based on the ideas and experiences of others in this field.

Ernst Wenk
Nora Harlow

INTRODUCTION

School crime and violence exploded into public view in the early 1970's with the hearings of the Senate Subcommittee to Investigate Juvenile Delinquency and the House Subcommittee on Elementary, Secondary, and Vocational Education. In releasing the preliminary report of the Senate Subcommittee, Senator Birch Bayh commented that a survey of public elementary and secondary schools had produced a "ledger of violence confronting our schools that reads like a casualty list from a war zone or a vice squad annual report." The relatively sudden appearance of a crime problem of this apparent magnitude and seriousness caught most Americans off-guard. The knowledge and experience needed to determine the causes of school crime or to design effective prevention programs simply were not available. School administrators had few guidelines for attempting to deal with what many of them viewed as the foremost problem of the nation's schools.

Since that time a number of nationwide studies have been undertaken to fill the need for information on school violence and vandalism. Results of the Safe School Study, conducted by the National Institute of Education (NIE), were published in December 1977. This important study, and a companion survey by the National Center for Education Statistics (NCES) in 1975, significantly expanded the knowledge base by providing information on the incidence and seriousness of crime in the schools, its costs, the number and location of schools affected, and prevention methods and their effectiveness.

Despite the growing knowledge base, school administrators may be overwhelmed by the complexity of the school crime problem, especially as it relates to youth crime in the community of which the school is a part. A simple categorization of five distinct strategies may be helpful when discussing the full range of prevention and intervention efforts which can be undertaken by a community or school. The five levels, envisioned as components of a comprehensive prevention program, represent increasingly serious consequences for the individual:

1. *Primary Action.* Primary action provides an *a priori* quality model for education and human services designed to enhance the students' lives.

2. *Primary Prevention.* This strategy focuses on children in need without identifying individuals as "delinquency-prone." Resources are provided to meet perceived needs without specific reference to delinquency prevention, although program priorities may be based on knowledge of the relationship between needs and social consequences.

3. *Prevention.* This level of intervention directly addresses individual children who are identified as in danger of becoming delinquent. At this stage, individuals or groups are "targeted" as they are diagnostically declared delinquency-prone.

4. *Treatment or Sanctions.* Efforts at this level are directed toward the overt manifestations of maladjustment that has become sufficiently intolerable to invoke response from school or community officials and that may lead to involvement in the justice system.

5. *Rehabilitation and Correction.* This strategy includes programs for the adjudicated delinquent returned to the community on probation or parole.

Within this framework, a school's prevention programs can be examined and evaluated and the absence of specific programs or services on any of these levels will be readily apparent. By filling in the gaps and eliminating unnecessary duplications in service, administrators can develop a comprehensive integrated overall strategy for the prevention and control of youth crime and misbehavior in the school and in the surrounding community. It is anticipated that this collection of papers will assist in such an undertaking.

CONTENTS

STUDYING SCHOOL CRIME:
A PRESCRIPTION FOR RESEARCH-BASED PREVENTION

John R. Garrett
Centre Research Associates
Newton Centre, MA

Scott A. Bass
Centre Research Associates
Newton Centre, MA

Michael D. Casserly
Centre Research Associates
Newton Centre, MA

There is no simple solution to the problem of violence and vandalism in any school. We know too little to generalize and the overarching theories are too global to be of real use. It is clear that research and action must be rooted in the unique characteristics of the particular school; yet we also must arrive, eventually, at a point where more general prescriptions are possible and one school or district can benefit from the experiences of others.

Current research on school crime has two primary weaknesses which impede the development of knowledge necessary to design effective prevention programs. First, there are no widely accepted criteria for identifying and recording various kinds of school crime. For example, in recording instances of vandalism, some school systems include certain categories of apparently accidental damage, while others do not; some include all destruction, while others include only acts for which a perpetrator is identified; some exclude damage covered by insurance, while others do not (1). The statistical impact of these differences is staggering. Clearly, common definitions and reporting criteria are needed if we are to begin to build reliable, testable theories that transcend individual schools and school systems.

Second, in addition to building a common data base on school crime, we need to begin constructing a framework of small-scale studies of individual school settings which will permit us to test, measure, and evaluate a variety of preventive approaches. In both the initial exploratory research and in evaluation of prevention programs we need to look not only at current problems but at the historical interactions which led to the present situation. Also required is an approach which focuses not only on "problem" students or schools but on the interface between the two. Neither the individual-oriented "medical" model nor the institutional-oriented determinist approach will adequately reveal the way in which the crime problem was generated or is perpetuated in any school or how it might best be controlled.

The primary difficulty with either approach in isolation arises from the unidimensionality of their respective arguments. The person-centered approach diverts attention from the role that groups and social arrangements play in determining choice among alternate behaviors; and the environmental perspective denies the individual's capacity to shape his own destiny. Neither explanation recognizes the importance of the dynamic interaction between the individual and society; neither describes the changes in both the individual and the institutions he confronts over time; and neither provides the practitioner with a clear indication of needed preventive action.

The following is offered as a potentially fruitful approach to the study of crime in schools and, building on the study results, to the design of programs to combat the school crime problem. It is hoped that other researchers and school practitioners will begin to obtain and report parallel findings, thus contributing to the construction of that core of setting-specific studies which is vital to the development of theory and its application in practice. The approach recommended here consists of five incremental steps: (1) site selection and study planning; (2) research (both individual and institutional); (3) presentation and discussion; (4) design and testing of preventive programs; and (5) measurement and reporting of results.

SITE SELECTION AND STUDY PLANNING

Interestingly, small-scale longitudinal studies leading to program development require much more careful site selection and planning than does more grandiose research. The relationships which develop between researchers and school staff, parents, and students are necessarily complex. In addition, the unfolding study process places significant and growing pressures on all parties, particularly the administrator in charge. These pressures are most intense, and most intensely resisted, when the findings of research begin to suggest solutions which require major alterations in school organization. Preparation and planning, therefore, must be carefully undertaken to avoid later disruption of the study process or resistance to program implementation.

First, it seems vital that top administrators and a few key teachers and parents perceive the problem as serious. This perception may not reflect the "real" incidence of school crime as revealed by reported statistics. However, without genuine concern on the part of influential school and community persons, the pressures generated by the study may become too much for the administrative structure to bear, especially when change is indicated. Second, the personal relationship between key researchers and key administrators is a critical factor in the success of small-scale longitudinal studies. Questions of access, influence, openness to change, and interpersonal support must be appraised before the study is initiated. Some information also is needed on relationships between the school and the community, between key school administrators and their supervisors in the school system, between teachers and administrators, and among administrators. Longitudinal studies and resulting programs are easily destroyed by changes in school or

13

community leadership — changes which frequently could have been predicted.

Once the study site has been selected, preparation and planning for research can begin. Because of profound differences among settings, generalizations are unlikely to be useful here. Nonetheless, all parties (including delinquent and nondelinquent youth, staff, administrators, parents, and members of the community) must understand what is going to happen, when it will happen, what will be expected of them, how they can contribute to the success of the study, and how and when they will receive information on study results. Needed as well are clear expressions of support for the project from responsible administrators, both in person and in writing.

Finally, all parties need to be encouraged to participate in the study process, providing ideas, reviewing suggestions, and generating alternatives. Early "ownership" by participants can be vital to success of a long-term study.

RESEARCH

Both offender-centered and institutional approaches seek to delineate the interchanges which occur within the school setting. One adopts and describes the perspective of delinquent youth; the other portrays the point of view of persons with formal institutional roles. The focus on interchanges from both perspectives seeks to conceptually break down the barriers between the person-centered and determinist approaches and to overcome some of the theoretical and methodological weaknesses of each.

The offender-based phase of the study is not intended primarily to identify delinquent youth who commit offenses. Instead, it is aimed at understanding and profiling the interchanges between youth and their school which lead to destructive and criminal behaviors. The approach is not clinical but epidemiological. A two-pronged investigation is used to explore school records and to interview identified delinquent and predelinquent

14

youth, as well as others who play significant roles in their lives. From these data, detailed case histories are developed describing an individual's "life path" within and outside the school setting, focusing on those events which appear to result in criminal behavior. Throughout, the data collected on individuals are used not to identify perpetrators, but to develop a clear perspective of behavior patterns within the school.

For purposes of investigation, four populations are identified as likely to be involved, or to have been involved, in criminal or destructive behavior: dropouts, chronic truants, chronic disciplinary cases, and individuals apprehended in cases of school-related crime. Systematic analyses of school, court, police, and other available records, abetted by interviews with representatives of each institution, should produce basic information on identified youth in each category. Principal questions for each include: Who are they (age, sex, residence, family status and mobility, ethnic group, physical disabilities, etc.)? What has happened to them (school performance, discipline, counseling, whether dropout or truant, previous police and court contacts or convictions, etc.)? Where are they now (employment, educational/training program, current counseling or police/court contacts or convictions, etc.)?

From these data, which are confidential and not identified with subjects' names, a profile of recorded history can be constructed for a representative sample of juveniles in the four target populations. Equally essential are the individual case histories which describe the life-path in greater detail from the point of view of the juvenile (tempered by information from relevant others). A random sample of each target population is selected for voluntary in-depth interviewing about their past experiences using a modified version of the "critical incident" technique (2). Events are identified in various social contexts (home, school, community, etc.) which the juvenile believes led to the present situation. These events, termed "critical junctures," are elaborated to include significant actors, settings, feelings and responses, what was said, and when and how it was said.

The interviewer may ask when and how the youth first got in trouble in school. Why? With whom? What happened as a result? How did it affect his family? His peers? Teachers and administrators? The purpose of these interviews is to develop a detailed description of identified critical junctures. For example, a confrontation in school may have led the youth to throw a rock through a classroom window and to his getting caught — "a critical juncture." This event would be detailed to show how, why, when, and where the youth threw the rock, who else was there, and what happened as a result.

Through the critical incident technique, descriptions of events are collected and coded showing the types, characteristics, and attributions of responses. At the same time, the data base retains the richness of descriptive personal accounts. It must be recognized, of course, that the events as reported by the youth may be colored by his desire to justify his actions and may bear little resemblance to reality. Once the critical junctures have been identified by the students as major points of movement toward delinquency, other key actors (teachers, peers, parents, administrators, police) are sought out and interviewed for their version of the event. In this way a more balanced set of case histories is assembled to complement the official record.

Data are collected and summarized for each of the target populations and for the group as a whole. Correlations among critical junctures for individuals in the study also are identified at this point to determine the similarity within and among target populations. These summary profiles, collected from the life-path data and focused on common critical junctures, become the foundation for the institutional phase of the study.

The institutional research phase parallels and builds upon the methodologies used and the results generated in developing the case histories and life paths of individual youths. The goal, in brief, is to identify key school "binding" processes which, from the institutional perspective, correlate positively with identified critical junctures. Detailed descriptions of these processes are developed by documenting policies, procedures, activities, and interactions of institutional representatives and students and creating a school profile.

As with the profile of the individual, a set of basic data about the school is collected. The record survey would elicit background data about the school setting and identified "binding" processes, including: Who was involved (number of students and their language, ethnicity and sex, and socioeconomic status, ethnicity and sex of staff, staff training, special class assignment)? What resources are available (curriculum and books, special and extracurricular programs, external support, available staff and volunteers, community programs, transportation, and support from other systems)? What are the constraints (location, physical structure and facility, attitudes of students, staff, and community, mandated programs, dropout and attendance rates, per-pupil expenditures, and problems unique to school and community)?

Again, the goal of the institutional assessment is not to identify "bad" staff or "wrong" school processes. This phase of research is designed instead to add substance to our understanding of the interactions which take place in schools. For example, if the counseling and placement process has been identified repeatedly as a critical juncture leading to delinquency for a significant number of youth, a careful look at the process should follow, including observations of counseling sessions, interviews with students and counselors involved, and general interviews with others in the school. Similar studies would be conducted for other "binding" processes (3) identified in prior phases of research. These data provide the basic input and outcome information on the particular school setting.

The second major component of the school profile is the process assessment, which examines the interchanges which take place around a "binding" process on a daily basis. This represents an in-depth version, from another vantage point, of institutional data to parallel previously gathered individual data. Primary school actors with personal affiliations to a "binding" school process are interviewed in depth to obtain their perceptions of the built-in constraints, conflicts, strengths, and limitations of the process. Perceived support from administrators and other professionals, use of resources, frustrations, workload, use of time, volume of paperwork, etc. are explored. The process also is observed in action in order to validate other sources of data and to provide a deeper understanding of how the process works for the various populations in the school. These observations focus on the interchanges which occur between other parties and students in the four high-risk target populations.

PRESENTATION AND DISCUSSION

The summarized results of both offender-centered and institutional phases of the research — focused on the "critical junctures" and "binding" processes identified and validated for the particular school — are presented separately to groups of youth in the target populations, other students, teachers, administrators, and parents and community representatives. Each group is asked to reflect on the research results and to determine whether the data agree with their own experience. In further discussions the groups separately attempt to develop alternative procedures or programs to improve student-institutional interchanges within each identified critical juncture or binding process.

As options are developed, the groups begin to merge in a "charette" process to develop and elucidate joint plans in identified problem areas. Because of the direct involvement of the school administration, it is anticipated that decision-makers' support for the programs developed is likely to be more readily available. The same is true of other community agencies and decision-makers who are directly involved in the program.

DEVELOPMENT AND TESTING OF
PREVENTIVE PROGRAMS

At this point, the program alternatives aimed at altering critical junctures and binding processes in the school are implemented and a new round of program development, evaluation, and alteration begins. It is important to note that program alternatives, however admirable, are not "solutions." As Seymour Sarason (4) has noted in another context, there are no solutions to social problems. Because of the vitality and movement of institutional life, all solutions lead, of necessity, to new sets of problems (binding processes) which will require new alternatives, which will generate new problems. The process of assessment, program development, evaluation and reassessment, therefore, must be ongoing if reductions in criminal and delinquent behavior are to be sustained.

MEASURING AND REPORTING RESULTS

In measuring the impact of alternative programs designed to prevent school crime, researchers need to insure comparability both within the system over time and across systems. When selecting measures of incidence, for example, both the statistical foundation existing in the system (as well as the logic, if any, which lies behind it) and national trends in related areas of data collection should be considered. Without comparable data, research can become either ahistorical or isolated from larger realities — all too common fates for educational evaluation.

In addition to looking at quantifiable indicators of crime and delinquency, program evaluators should continue to collect information on the interchange variables as was done in the initial study. The real impact of a program aimed at reducing school crime is qualitative as well as quantitative and should be revealed in altered and improved interactions among all parties in the school.

Finally, as the process continues, ongoing research will reveal new critical junctures and binding processes which should lead to new programs aimed at altering individual and institutional arrangements. In school settings at least, experience suggests that while change is constant and improvement possible, permanent solutions are not. And, for all those living and working in that complex, exciting, and frustrating web of relationships we call school, this is just as well.

19

FOOTNOTES

1. A national review of programs to reduce school vandalism has been conducted by the authors for the Council of the Great City Schools. The final product appears as an LEAA Prescriptive Package, published in Fall 1978.
2. Flanagan, J., "Critical Incident Technique," PSYCHOLOG-ICAL BULLETIN, 1954, Vol. 51, pp. 327-358.
3. The "binding" processes will vary from one setting to another. Examples drawn from previous work include: classroom placement, special placement, classroom discipline, central office discipline, lunchroom control, hallway control, physical education activities, peer interactions, out-of-building conflicts, home and neighborhood, among others.
4. Sarason, S., THE CULTURE OF THE SCHOOL AND THE PROBLEM OF CHANGE (Boston: Allyn and Bacon, Inc., 1971).

THE SOCIAL ORGANIZATION OF THE HIGH SCHOOL:

SCHOOL-SPECIFIC ASPECTS OF SCHOOL CRIME

Francis A. J. Ianni
Horace Mann-Lincoln Institute
Teachers College, Columbia University

In responding to the problem of violence and vandalism in the schools, it is tempting to ignore the possibility of school-specific aspects of school crime and to look for explanations, and solutions, in what we think we know about crime rather than in what we think we know about schools. As a result, we are likely to view school crime from the same personal and institutional perspectives which have failed to control crime in the rest of society. Yet violence and disruption in schools does differ from crime in the streets, not only because it disrupts the learning process and diverts resources intended for educational purposes to pay for crime control, but also because, through the socialization process which takes place in schools, it can have a lasting effect on youth which spreads outward from the school over time.

Viewing school crime within the context of the school is not, however, an easy task. The boundaries between the school and the family, the school and the community, or the school and the media are unclear, making it difficult to say where formal schooling begins or ends. Researchers commonly have focused on individual students as learners, giving little attention to the social organization of learning or the ways in which such educating systems intersect with the formal organization of the school. Research on schools as organizations has come largely from a concern with administration and management rather than education and so intersects instead with the literature on the organization of business and government.

Consequently, while we know something about how children behave as learners and are beginning to get some ideas about how adults organize and manage schools as places to work, we know very little about how schools operate as social systems. We know even less about the types of social control which relate children and adults into learning and socialization structures within the school or how these function to promote or hinder learning and the socialization process. Yet it is here that are found the answers to complex questions about the role of schools in producing, aggravating, or reducing school crime; how schools mediate between students and other components of the social system; and whether and how changes in school organization and operation can remedy the problem we call school crime.

RESEARCH ON SCHOOL ORGANIZATION

Since early 1972, a group of anthropologists and educators with previous experience in both educational and criminal justice research has been developing a model of the social organization of the American high school. This model is designed to provide a school-specific focus for examining a number of socio-educational problems, including school crime and violence. The focus has been on schools as social systems which operate according to an observable code of rules specific to the school rather than generally analogous to those of other institutional settings.

In the sense that the term "rules" is used here, it describes a control mechanism which regulates and regularizes relationships both within the school and between the school and the outside world. It is this code of rules which keeps the school functioning as an educating and socializing system and which structures behavior for individual and group safety and security. Control systems of this sort begin by defining what is "good" and what is "bad," what is expected and what is condemned, and result in specific rules which operationalize these definitions and apply them to everyday situations. As a totality, these rules form a behavioral code which is manifested and observable in their behavior.

Since this code appears to be the key to understanding how schools function as social systems, the central question in the research reported here has been: "What is the code of rules which makes the high school a social system and how do people learn to play this game?" In the first phase of the study (1972-1973) three teams of ethnographers studied three high schools simultaneously, using the same field methods and constantly comparing the data gathered in each of the schools (1). The three schools covered a rural/suburban/inner-city continuum in the metropolitan area of New York and New Jersey.

One of the schools is located in a small, up-state New York town drawing from a catchment area which includes several small rural townships. It has a student population of about 700. The second school is in an upper-middle-class New Jersey suburb composed chiefly of single family dwellings occupied by commuting executives and their families. This school has about 600 students. Student and teacher populations of both schools are primarily white Protestant (with some Roman Catholic admixture). The third school, located in a multi-ethnic area of New York City, has a student population of 4,400 divided among Hispanics, blacks, Chinese, and a "white" group which, while predominantly Italian and Jewish, also contains a number of other ethnic and religious groups. There are subdivisions within each of these primary groups; for example, Hong Kong-born as contrasted to American-born Chinese or Chinese from mainland China and West Indian as contrasted to American-born blacks. Most of the teachers in this school are white.

Each of the field teams lived in the community of the school they studied and were in the schools every day. Since these schools were to be viewed as "free standing" social systems, an effort was made to avoid traditional paradigms of school structure and to study the classroom and school milieus as interactive rather than separate units of observation and analysis. Eventually, the study was expanded to include the periphery of the school and the community as well. Since from previous experience it was known that interactive behavior sometimes starts in the classroom and then flows out into the halls and even outside the school (or, alternately, moves into the school from outside), it was considered desirable to follow that flow of action wherever it led.

"Events" in the schools were selected as units of observation and analysis (again, rather than "classrooms" or "teacher-student interactions"), since these are spontaneous and not deduced logically from what already is known about the organization of high schools. Throughout the study, two kinds of events were observed, recorded, and analyzed: (1) recurrent events which regularize daily life in the schools and (2) those unpredictable occurrences which disrupt that regularity and sometimes change the course of activity to such an extent that they lead to new regularities. These events — ranging from routine activities such as taking attendance to more dramatic ones such as a shoot-out in the cafeteria — were followed wherever they led.

The individuals involved in each event were identified and interviewed in an attempt to understand the event from the perspective of those who participated in it as well as from the outside observer's point of view. These interviews were plotted to indicate who did what, when, and where; the identity of both actors and observers and the roles they played; and, where conflicting perceptions of the same event indicated differences among types of participants, the nature of those different groups. At a later stage of the research (1975), a number of life histories were added to provide some longitudinal comparisons regarding the ways in which recurrent events structured students' and teachers' lives and how unpredictable events affected the regularities of the school cycle.

SOCIAL ORGANIZATION OF THE HIGH SCHOOL: A MODEL

From analyses of field notes on the three high schools studied, a model of the social organization of the high school was constructed. This model assumes that the major functions of the school are organized into four structural domains: the teaching-learning structure; the authority-power structure; the peer group structure; and cross-group structures. Each of these structures describes a different area of enculturation and specific pattern of socialization for adults as well as children (2). The *teaching-learning* structure organizes the enculturation of cognitive and affective skills which define the learning function of the school. Since socialization is considered transactional, this structure includes the interaction patterns through which teachers are socialized to the learning style valued by the school as well as the school's definition of the child's role in the learning function. When a school is described as "academically-oriented" or "achievement-oriented" it is the teaching-learning structure, and the roles of teachers and students within it, which is being described.

The *authority-power structure* describes the enculturation of disciplines, authority, and power of adults and adult-controlled institutional complexes (government, the world of work, and so on). Socialization within this structure is organized by compulsory attendance laws, age-grading of both student and adult populations of the school, the governance process within the school and the classroom, and the quasi-governmental auspices of the school-community relationship (where rules governing teachers as well as students and patterns of resource allocation are dictated by outsiders). When a school is described as "in-control," as opposed to one which is chaotic or out-of-control, it is the authority-power structure which is being described. The notion of a "turn-around" school, for example, describes one in which the authority-power structure has been re-established or reinforced.

The *peer-group structure* refers to the enculturation of group values and norms in the two distinct peer groups in the high school, that of child and that of adult. The values and behaviors particular to each of these groups are, to some extent, generation-bound, but they also differ because they take place within the school. Peer-group socialization involves learning to get along with each other (among teachers as well as among students), but it also involves learning roles, establishing patterns of conflict and agreement, and defining group values and behavioral expectations. Differences in group definitions represent more than the so-called "generation gap;" they are affected as well by ethnic and social class differences between staff and student populations.

Cross-group structures refer to the enculturation of behavior codes for interaction between the two peer groups, including definitions of mediator roles and communication styles. Here socialization defines how teachers and students relate to each other; it considers the rights and responsibilities of each and includes some school safety concerns (such as student respect for teachers' authority and how it is to be expressed). Of considerable importance, but often ignored, is the process of mediation between the two groups. Mediator roles can be formal (e.g., counselors, students appointed to governance committees, deans of discipline or of students, and even homeroom teachers). Many informal roles, however, also emerge in the pattern of relationships established in the schools. The mediating role of "coach," for example, does not follow the traditional teacher-student role set, nor does the role of teacher-advisor of special interest clubs. Informal mediating relationships also may be based on ethnicity in schools with a majority of black, Hispanic, or other "minority" youngsters and a small number of teachers from those same groups (3).

Each of these four structures is associated with a characteristic process. While the "structure" actually is a network of relationships among individuals which are defined by legal and administrative, group and individual decisions, the "process" represents patterns of behavior which channel or mold communications and behaviors among these individuals. Teachers, for example, usually talk differently to each other than they do to students; but they also talk differently within the teaching-learning structure than they do when they are within the authority-power structure. Students also behave differently within the different structures.

Research to date has identified three major processes of social action by which the four structures are operationalized in the daily life of a school and which adjust those structures to changing demographic, political, social, and economic conditions. These processes were observed with such regularity in each of the schools studied that they appear to be basic to the organization of social interaction within and across the four major structures in all schools.

The first of these is the process of *sorting* in which individuals classify themselves and each other according to a set of culturally defined labels. While the labels may vary from school to school, the process of sorting is fundamental to the pattern of social relationships in every school. Students "sort" each other and are "sorted" by teachers and administrators. Discrepancies between the sorting process used by students and that used by adults can lead to tensions and conflicts which jeopardize school safety. Changes in the sorting process over time may indicate positive or negative interpretations of the teaching-learning or authority-power structures by modifying the pattern of social relations within a particular school.

For example, a "turn-around" school, which at one time had a predominantly white student and teacher population, underwent a steady decline in both academic and disciplinary characteristics over a five-year period as increasing numbers of black and Hispanic children entered the school. The teachers and administrators in the school, still the same white group from the earlier period, attributed the change to the influx of black and Hispanic children who were seen (sorted) as uneducable and violent. When a new community-selected principal sought out capable black and Hispanic children throughout his district and arranged for them to transfer to this school, he changed the mix of students with some obvious effects on the sorting process. The teachers were impressed by the new students and "black" and "Hispanic" no longer were equated with "uneducable and violent." The change in the sorting process also affected the student peer-group structure: ethnicity no longer served as the only basis for clique formation and cross-ethnic cliques based on mutual interest began to form.

The second major process of social action is *territoriality*. This refers to the formal and informal assignment of space within the school, access to particular school groups, and the effects of particular school environments (e.g., the classroom as opposed to the cafeteria) on behavior. Size of school also is a function of territoriality in both absolute and relative terms. For example, it was found that the urban school, which was far larger than the suburban or rural school, was characterized by a qualitatively different social environment resulting as much from its size as its urban location. When the population of the urban school decreased from 5,500 to 4,400, the "crowding factor," which can be a cause of tensions in schools, was considerably reduced.

Finally, the process of *rule-making and rule-breaking* serves as a third means of organizing behavior within the four major structures. In the school environment there is a continual proliferation of rules, yet rule enforcement varies widely from one school to another. Differences may exist across categories (such as teacher or student), between different enforcers or offenders, over time, or from one place to another. All of the factors which cause rules to be made in particular situations, and which determine whether or not they are enforced, provide indicators of the social organization of the school.

Collectively, the processes which mold and channel behavior within the four structures are expressed as behavioral expectations which set the limits for approved behavior in the school. This loose collection of shared understandings which, while not codified, limits the variability of permissible behavior, might be called the school "charter." This charter represents the formal component of what is usually considered the informal social organization of the high school. A teacher generally will allow an individual student a certain degree of freedom of behavior in the classroom before invoking the charter to describe (and sanction) the expected behavior for students in the teaching-learning structure, in the authority-power structure, or, in some cases, in both. Similarly, the principal will allow some variability in teacher behavior before he invokes the charter.

Interestingly, the charter is invoked as frequently, and possibly more frequently, by a lower person or group to sanction a higher one as it is by a person in a position of power to sanction a subordinate. Also, since both teachers and administrators generally seem to be reluctant to make decisions and absolute rules which might set a pattern of enforcement (4), much of the daily life of the school proceeds from the shared understandings of the charter rather than from specific rules. The process of invocation thus comes to represent the primary mechanism of social control within the school.

Figure 1 displays the relationships among the four major structures, the processes of sorting, territoriality, and rule-making and rule-breaking, and the school charter.

SCHOOL CRIME AND THE SOCIAL ORGANIZATION MODEL

The model presented here offers a means of looking at school crime and violence by isolating what is school-specific from more general societal factors. Some of the schools studied were found to be more physically secure than the surrounding neighborhoods. In fact, parents of students in one such school reported that they felt at ease while their children were in school and became concerned only when they were travelling to and from school. Clearly, the assumption that violent communities produce violent schools does not consider the fact that school climate and community climate do not always coincide. In the three high schools studied, violent crimes (assaults, extortion backed by physical threat, knifings and shootings) were significantly more common in the urban school than they were in either the suburban or the rural school. While this appears to reaffirm the widespread notion that levels of crime in the community are reflected in the school, further analysis revealed that most of the violence actually occurred in the

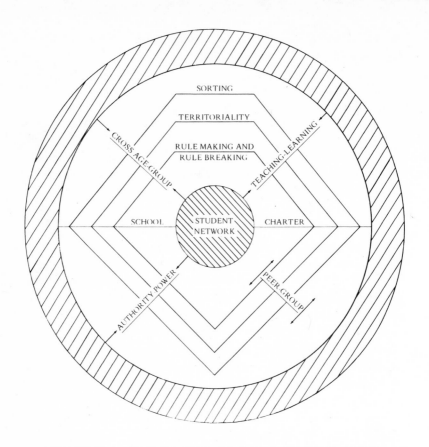

FIGURE 1: THE SOCIAL ORGANIZATION OF THE HIGH SCHOOL

community rather than the school. Compared to the community in which it was located, there was less violence in this school even when only those crimes by and against high-school age students were considered.

There are a number of possible explanations for this phenomenon. One is that youth spend more time in the community than they do in the school. Another is that crimes committed in the community are more likely to be reported to the police. However, the findings of this study suggest that the difference is due instead to the ordering of relationships and the type and extent of social control found in the school. When the three high schools were compared, variations in school crime and discipline were found to be more responsive to changes in the social organizations of the school than could be accounted for by variations in community characteristics. The community certainly is a major determinant of the social organization of a particular school, but the patterns of relationships made possible by that social organization intervene to structure individual and collective behavior. This was found to be true for each of the three processes of sorting, territoriality, and the making and breaking of rules.

The sorting process was found to operate in each of the schools studied, but the basis for sorting differed in each school. In the rural school, which is a consolidated high school drawing students from a number of rural townships, students are sorted according to where they live. Students from one township, for example, are considered "hell-raisers," while students from another are described as "well-behaved" and "serious students." In the urban school, which draws students from different sections of the city, where one lives is less important than ethnicity as a basis for sorting. Blacks are identified by teachers as potentially violent and teachers often ignore charter violations or even obvious rule violations in order to avoid a confrontation. Hispanics also are considered potentially violent, but in this case the various sub-groupings are important to the sorting process. Puerto Ricans, for example, are described as "highly verbal," even "loquatious" to the point that teachers character-ize their style as "talking you to death," while Domincans are considered "irrationally violent" and, like blacks, to be avoided. Of all groups in this school, the Chinese are considered the most disciplined as well as the best students. Here again, however, students from Hong Kong are considered to be better students than mainland Chinese because "their schools are more like ours." In the suburban school, where students are ethnically and socioeconomically homogeneous, neither community of origin nor ethnicity is a basis for sorting. Here students are sorted into two major groupings of "jocks," school-spirited students, and "freaks" (those considered socially deviant from

31

that spirit). School officials maintain that "freaks" are much more likely to become discipline problems and to violate drug laws than are "jocks."

Whether ethnicity, community of origin, or some other basis is used for sorting individuals into categories of "violence-prone," "discipline problems," or any other label denoting deviance, there are school-specific problems associated with sorting. An obvious problem is that if, as labeling theorists claim, labels communicate behavioral expectations to the labelled individual or group, then problems of discipline and crime may be intensified, if not actually instigated, by sorting (5). However, a more certain educational problem is that, despite any public posturing to the contrary, schools use these sorting categories as a basis for placing students in the teaching-learning structure as well as in the authority-power structure. This has important implications for social action programs, such as desegregation, which attempt to change the mix of students in a school, but it also bears significantly on school crime and discipline. Black students in the urban high school, for example, not only lose out in terms of socialization because, as "potentially violent," they are ignored when they violate the school charter; they also lose out in terms of enculturation because they are tracked into programs which do little to produce cultural competence. The potential for violence and crime in this double-bind is obvious; yet the school, more easily than the local community or the larger society, could adjust its sorting process to correct such problems since it does control the teaching-learning structure.

The process of territoriality also provides a means of viewing school safety within the context of the school. The anonymity provided by the large size of the urban school is an obvious factor in its significantly higher rates of misbehavior and crime as compared to the much smaller rural and suburban schools (6). Conversely, in both rural and suburban schools, teachers know most of the students and so can immediately recognize misbehaving students. Even more important, the students know that they will be recognized. There is, however, a more positive aspect of the relationship between school size and school safety. Integration into school activities and programs is more easily accomplished in smaller rural and suburban schools, not only because of the more personalized nature of relationships in the cross-age group structure, but because the peer structure provides greater opportunities for informal relations as well. The physical size of the large urban school observed in this study made it impossible for students to relate to the school as a totality. Student groups, sorted by ethnicity, established control over particular stairwells in the school and even over "turfs" on the sidewalks outside in much the same manner as prisoners set up "courts" or territories in prison yards (7). These territorial claims not only reduce interaction among ethnic groups, but also provide a source of potential conflict and violence (8).

Finally, the making and breaking of rules is one of the most important school-specific factors in crime and violence which must be examined in designing responses to the problem of school safety. In all three schools studied, the order or social control exercised by the administration – particularly the principal – was a major factor in the level of crime and violence in the school. Specifically, the less ambiguity in the authority-power structure (i.e., the smaller the tendency to allow some groups of individuals under some circumstances or at some times to violate certain rules or to ignore the limits set by the charter), the greater the sense of order and control in the school. In the urban school, for example, the principal had spent the past five years bringing order to a once chaotic school by applying uncompromising control over student behavior and, as much as possible, teacher behavior as well. The school is now "in control" and is considered a turn-around school by the central school board officials. Of course, a high price often is paid in the teaching-learning structure for the order established in the authority-power structure. Teachers and administrators, however, are quick to point out that the costs of crime in school may be high enough to warrant the price.

CONCLUSION

Schools play a distinctive role in the school crime problem which is demonstrably different from that of the family, the community, or society in general. Regardless of the contribution of the school to the problem of school-based violence and crime, there seems little question that crime presents unique problems when it occurs in the school. In addition to the human and property costs of crime, it inevitably disrupts the learning function, depletes resources intended for educational purposes, and negatively affects the socialization process with the likely result of increasing youthful violence and disruption both in school and in the larger society.

If there is insufficient evidence to argue that the school does cause or aggravate its own problems with disruption and crime, there is even less to answer the question of whether schools can be left to deal with these problems in their own way. Certainly the traditional reliance on the school as the primary medium for resolving social problems is no longer tenable. We may never be able to "teach" solutions to the problem of school crime as part of the school's curriculum. We can, nonetheless, introduce changes in the social organization of schools by altering the ways in which students are sorted, adjusting territoriality by attending to such matters as school size and design, and re-examining the manner in which school rules are made and enforced. Such changes, which appear likely to impact the school crime problem in many districts, also have the not inconsiderable advantage of being within the school's own span of control and thus requiring no drastic societal adjustments.

FOOTNOTES

1. In the second phase of the study (1975-1978) field work has concentrated on a number of specific problems such as desegregation and drug abuse. Also under study are violence and vandalism in a number of similar schools in the New York City area.

2. Learning and adaptation take place through both encultura- tion and socialization, but the source of what is learned as well as the learning process differs in each case. The concept of enculturation describes the cultural conditioning through which individuals are taught standardized responses to cultural stimuli. Essentially, this is a one-way process of cultural trans- mission through which the school attempts to produce culturally competent individuals. Socialization, on the other hand, can be seen as transactional, describing the process by which the individual (adult as well as child) is integrated with the social organization of the school and community under study. See Herskovits, M. J., CULTURAL ANTHROPOLOGY (New York: Knopf, 1948), pp. 326-7.

3. In many urban areas, school custodial staff, security guards, cafeteria workers, and other personnel tend to approximate the ethnic and social-class background of students more closely than teachers.

4. This confirms an earlier finding by McPherson, G., SMALL TOWN TEACHER (Cambridge, Mass.: Harvard University Press, 1972), p. 153.

5. Becker, S. OUTSIDERS: STUDIES IN THE SOCIOLOGY OF DEVIANCE (New York: Free Press, 1963); and Schur, E. M., LABELLING DEVIANT BEHAVIOR (New York: Harper and Row, 1971).

6. Barker, R. G. and Gump, P. V., BIG SCHOOL, SMALL SCHOOL: HIGH SCHOOL SIZE AND STUDENT BEHAVIOR (Stanford, Calif.: Stanford University Press, 1963).

7. Ianni, F. A. J., BLACK MAFIA: ETHNIC SUCCESSION

IN ORGANIZED CRIME (New York: Simon and Schuster, 1976).

8. Interestingly, the territories or "turfs" claimed by student groups are not often the locus of violence. The crimes which occur there tend to be victimless crimes such as drug use or selling rather than violence which would bring "heat" and jeopardize the availability of the student-controlled space.

SCHOLASTIC EXPERIENCES, SELF-ESTEEM AND DELINQUENT BEHAVIOR: A THEORY FOR ALTERNATIVE SCHOOLS

Martin Gold
Institute for Social Research
The University of Michigan

Delinquent behavior is an ego defense, in the psychoanalytic meaning of that term (1), against external realities which threaten a young person's self-esteem (2). A derogated self-image is naturally aversive and it will set in motion psychic forces to dispel it. Delinquent behavior is such a psychological defense in that it provides a way of avoiding situations which endanger self-esteem and of engaging in experiences that promise a form of self-enhancement. A situation endangering self-esteem can be regarded as a *provocation* to delinquency: it is an experience that motivates an individual to be disruptive and delinquent.

One important setting in a young person's life which is rife with provocations to delinquent behavior is the school. Incompetence or failure in school can be seen as a major provocation to delinquent behavior. Achievement is the core of the student role in American society, and in no other role are the standards of achievement so clear or the means to attain them so narrow. Experiences of success and failure pervade scholastic life (3). If an adolescent falls short of his aspirations for scholastic achievement, and if he experiences few if any other successes in school life (such as popularity with peers or athletic achievement), he will have to cope in some way with a lowered self-image.

Disruptive or delinquent behavior in school is especially appropriate as a way of coping with low self-esteem for several reasons. First, the behavior occurs at the time and in the place

37

where the pain of failure is felt. Second, the appreciative audience that enhances its effectiveness as a coping mechanism is more readily found at school then elsewhere. Typically there is an undercurrent of adolescent negativity toward school, even among students who would not behave badly themselves, which provides a wide audience for such behavior. And, third, while disruptive behavior in school functions as a public performance or a mode of self-presentation, it is also a declaration of revolt against the criteria by which the youth has come to regard himself as a failure. It defies the exercise of authority over both deportment and standards for scholastic achievement; it devalues the devaluations and the devaluators (4).

Usually, however, an individual also has strong controls — some goals and values — which constrain him from acting delinquent in response to provocations. Not every youth who is failing as a student finds disruptive or delinquent behavior an appropriate way to rescue his or her self-esteem. Some youngsters are so closely attached to people who discourage such behavior that the support offered by an audience of their peers is offset by adult disapproval. Parents, of course, are the primary sources of such control. Where there are warm parent-adolescent relationships that might be ruptured; where there is love that might be withdrawn; where there are affectional, material, and other resources that might be withheld; disruptive behavior is not displayed because it bears more costs than benefits.

When strong controls effectively counter strong provocations to be disruptive, delinquency is not a defense against a derogated self-image. Unable to cope by engaging in disruptive and delinquent behavior, a youth is likely to feel a great deal of anxiety and may take flight from reality, depending on the availability of other coping skills and the presence of other forces in his life. Alternatives to disruptive and delinquent behavior may include various forms of mental illness, particularly pervasive anxiety.

Since the schools create situations which endanger self-esteem, they are regarded as powerful determinants of delinquent behavior; that is, they control major social and psychological forces which generate it. While other social institutions also play some part in producing delinquency (e.g., the family, the economy, the juvenile justice system, the mass media), the role of the school can be considered independently. Alternative educational programs which maximize success experiences thus have the potential to reduce the provocations for and strengthen the controls against delinquency (5).

SUPPORTING EVIDENCE

Credence to the theoretical model briefly sketched above is provided by evidence scattered throughout the social science literature. Since no single study provides data on all the hypothetical links, the literature must be drawn upon piecemeal as it casts some light on one link or another or as it demonstrates the effect of a particular component of an alternative school program.

Results of research, for example, leave little doubt that better students tend to have higher self-esteem. Studies employing a variety of measures of both scholastic competence and self-esteem have demonstrated this relationship (6). The relationship between scholastic achievement and disruptive or delinquent behavior, on the other hand, cannot be documented by research that relies on official records of apprehended, adjudicated, and incarcerated youth. Since an official record is more often acquired when a youth's school record is poor, the relationship with academic deficiency is built into the delinquency data by the juvenile justice system.

However, studies measuring delinquent behavior by means of unofficial observations and self reports support the hypothesis that, compared to their more successful counterparts, poor school achievers are more likely to be involved in incidents of disruptive behavior in school (7). Disruptive students identified by teachers tend to score lower in reading and arithmetic tests throughout high school, regardless of socioeconomic background (8). When the frequency of self-reported delinquent behavior is correlated with teachers' ratings of class rank in scholastic achievement, the same relationship is revealed (9). This relationship does not confirm causation, however, and further research should be directed toward investigating whether or not delinquent behavior declines when academic record improves.

Studies examining the relationship between self-esteem and delinquent behavior do suggest a causal relationship: low self-esteem generates or leads to delinquency (10). For example, in a predictive study of 4,000 junior high school students, Kaplan found that more of those who had evinced low self-esteem at the beginning of the school year reported having committed each of 22 deviant acts during the ensuing year than did those who had indicated high self-esteem (11).

The hypothesis usually tested in research relating anxiety to academic record is that high anxiety interferes with scholastic achievement. The theoretical approach presented above, however, posits a causal relationship in the opposite direction: low achievement should increase anxiety. Research findings generally support the association between high anxiety and low academic achievement (12). More anxious students (as measured by self-reports of tension and teachers' ratings of anxiety) score lower on standard achievement tests than do those exhibiting little anxiety (13).

We have suggested that because delinquency is an effective defense against a derogated self-image it should be negatively related to (i.e., it should reduce) anxiety. Although relevant data are sparse and the theory itself is ambiguous on the appropriateness of the various measures of anxiety employed, youth defined as delinquent generally prove to be less anxious (14). However, whether disruptive and delinquent behavior may shield adolescents from anxiety is less certain; the theory and the appropriate measures are not yet precise enough to support a firm conclusion.

AN ALTERNATIVE EDUCATIONAL PROGRAM

The school has been shown to function independently from

other social institutions in determining delinquency. Practically speaking, then, the school can mount an ameliorative effort which may prove effective in reducing delinquency regardless of other influences on disruptive youth. The educational program outlined herein is designed for youth who are disruptive in the school and the community and whose behavior may plausibly be supposed to stem from their failures as students.

Two essential ingredients of such an alternative education program are: (1) a significant increase in the proportion of a youth's experiences of success over failure; and (2) provision of a warm, accepting relationship with one or more adults. Both of these point to the need for a program which tailors the educational process to the individual in several ways. First, the educational materials and tasks must be appropriate to the student's present level of skills. Second, their content must appeal to the student's own interests. Third, the student must be allowed to master them at his or her own pace. And fourth, progress should be evaluated solely on the basis of individual performance rather than on the standard criteria established in accordance with the norms for age or grade.

The social norms which typically govern formal role relationships between teacher and student must be largely suspended in an alternative program and replaced by more informal interpersonal relations. Ordinarily, secondary school teachers are encouraged to assume a routine pleasantness toward their students that amounts to an affective neutrality. In the interests of fairness, teacher-student relationships are governed by universalistic principles which are fairly constant from one student to another. Neither teacher nor student is supposed to take the other's peculiarities into account in the enactment of his respective role.

Interpersonal relations, in contrast, are affectively loaded relationships in which participants demonstrate their changing feelings toward one another. Each takes into account the other's individuality in their interactions rather than abiding by the more strict rules of a formal relationship. An effec-

41

tive alternative education teacher thus should create a unique relationship with each student, a relationship into which is infused a genuine liking and acceptance of the student but which does not conceal genuine revulsion for some kinds of behavior.

It is suggested that a program with these ingredients would reduce the provocation of school failure by providing successful experiences. The warm, accepting relationship with teachers presumably would enhance the student's self-image and, at the same time, would encourage the formation of social bonds which strengthen the individual's controls over his own behavior. Such programs already have evolved independently of any explicit theory. Descriptions of alternative school programs for delinquent youth often emphasize individualized curricula, ungraded classrooms, personal evaluation, and warm teacher-student relationships. Swidler describes two alternative high schools in Berkeley, California, which stress these ingredients:

> Group High and Ethnic High avoided teaching students about achievement, about success and failure. They concentrated instead on teaching students self-confidence and self-respect. The first element in increasing self-confidence was reducing the inequality of status between teachers and students. Casual, friendly relations between teachers and students lessened students' fear, and made the teachers seem approachable, non-intimidating friends. ...A second way to avoid evaluating students, and to build self-confidence is to construct assignments with few possibilities for failure.... Students were praised and rewarded for 'sharing their ideas' with the group, not for having the right answers (15).

But with these as with other efforts to reduce delinquency, data rarely are collected to test either the effectiveness of the program or the accuracy of its theoretical assumptions. An examination of the available data permits certain conclusions regarding separate components of the proposed program: from this, a prognosis for its successful implementation as a delinquency reducing strategy may be projected.

The data relating to the two essential components of an effective alternative school program — increasing the ratio of success/failure experiences and establishing warm interpersonal relationships with norm-abiding adults — are supportive in that delinquent behavior generally is reduced where such strategies are employed. For example, in a Quincy, Illinois, alternative school program reported by Bowman (16), 60 eighth graders who were performing poorly in school and who were discipline problems were selected for study. Three groups of 20 students were defined randomly. Two groups constituted special classes while the students in the third continued in the conventional junior high school program. In the alternative program, students spent a larger share of their school day with one teacher who had volunteered to lead the class, who knew the students well, and who was sympathetic toward them. These children were not pushed to achieve; the pace was slow, tailored to their current levels of functioning. Clearly the intent of the program was to maximize success experiences and provide warm interpersonal relationships between teachers and students.

The effects of this program were mixed but promising. The students in the alternative program showed neither more nor less gain in achievement scores than the randomized controls. But their attitudes toward school and their attendance rates improved relative to the controls. About two years after the program began, official delinquency records were checked again, revealing that the students in the alternative program had had fewer contacts with the police, and the offenses for which they were apprehended had become less serious. The control group exhibited the opposite trend, more in line with expectations for youth as they enter their fifteenth and sixteenth years. Although it is not clear from the published reports what produced the positive changes, it seems likely that increased social bonds with their teachers provided students with some constraints against antisocial behavior. Although there was no objective improvement in the scholastic achievement of the experimental students, it can be assumed that these students believed their performance was improving. This study thus can be seen as lending support to the hypothesis that subjective experiences of success in school lead to a reduction in delinquent behavior. It also may be assumed that, in most cases, objective improvement would induce subjective experiences of progress.

The importance of a warm relationship with a socializing adult in the effective treatment of delinquents also is underlined by Persons and Pepinsky (17) who found impressive differential follow-up records for two randomized groups of incarcerated boys after they were released to their communities. After the same amount of time on the outside, 61 percent of the control group were re-institutionalized for delinquent behavior, compared to 32 percent of the experimental group which had participated in a psychotherapeutic program that encouraged "warm, interpersonal relationships, both with the therapist and with the other boys..." (p. 530). Another more recent study found that the establishment of interpersonal relationships was a key to changing the behavior of disruptive and delinquent adolescents (as measured by lowered recidivism rates) (18).

NEED FOR ADDITIONAL RESEARCH

The two ingredients hypothesized for alternative school programs must be realized in concrete programs before confident evaluations can be made. Administrative orientations must be changed, teachers selected and trained, learning materials assembled, sites established, and students identified. Program evaluation should take the form of a rigorous field experiment which not only assesses the degree to which a program reaches its goal of delinquency reduction but also tests whether the theory is valid. That is, an experiment must first determine whether, as compared to conventional school programs, a program actually raises the ratio of scholastic successes over failures and establishes warmer interpersonal relationships between students and teachers. Research should then determine whether these elements actually affect students' self-esteem. Finally, it should be determined whether or not raising levels of self-esteem, especially on unconscious levels, lowers delinquent behavior.

In the process of implementing and evaluating alternative programs, several practical questions will have to be addressed for which theory does not suggest answers. One is where an alternative program should be located — whether in close contact with a conventional secondary school or isolated from it. On the one hand, affinity with a conventional school may facilitate re-entry of students to the mainstream, with which they should learn to cope and to which they eventually will have to return, if not in school then later in employment. On the other hand, the desirability of building an *esprit* among the students and staff of an alternative school and the problems of dealing with students' behavior early in their experience with the program favor relative isolation.

Another question which must be answered by experience and experimentation has to do with the identification and recruitment of students. Should students be assigned to the alternative programs as they typically are assigned to a home-room or should their recruitment be entirely voluntary? Should the program recruit problem students exclusively or should there be a mix of prosocial and antisocial students? Involved in these questions are issues of labeling and stigmatization and the potential effectiveness of imposed intervention, however benign.

A third question has to do with program failure. How far and for how long can an alternative school tolerate a recalcitrant youth? Can gradations of inclusion-exclusion be established within a program so that differences among students can be accommodated? What is the next alternative to an alternative program? Should the power to exclude a youth from a public school system rest with the school system or should it be exercised by the juvenile justice system?

Although these questions are complex and cannot be answered here, one guiding principle can be specified: solutions conducive to reform, of both individuals and institutions, must take into account not only their effect on youths' self-esteem but also their potential for helping youth find a respectable place in their community and in society.

FOOTNOTES

1. Freud, A., THE EGO AND MECHANISMS OF DEFENSE (New York: International Universities Press, 1946).
2. Delinquent behavior is defined, for the purposes of this paper, as the deliberate commission by a juvenile of an act he/she knows violates the juvenile code in such a way that if he/she is caught, he/she is liable to judicial response. It is measured by self-report data and not by official records of juvenile offenses. See Gold, M., DELINQUENT BEHAVIOR IN AN AMERICAN CITY (Belmont, Cal.: Brooks/Cole, 1970), and Gold, M. and Mann, D., "Delinquency as defense," AMERICAN JOURNAL OF ORTHOPSYCHIATRY, (42): 463-379, 1972.
3. Glasser, W., SCHOOLS WITHOUT FAILURE (New York: Harper and Row, 1969).
4. Cohen, A., DELINQUENT BOYS: THE CULTURE OF THE GANG (New York: Free Press, 1955).
5. Short, J. F., Jr., and Strodtbeck, F. L., GROUP PROCESS AND GANG DELINQUENCY (Chicago: University of Chicago Press, 1965). These authors arrived at similar conclusions from their study of peer processes in delinquent behavior.
6. Bachman, J. G., YOUTH IN TRANSITION: (Vol. II) THE IMPACT OF FAMILY BACKGROUND AND INTELLIGENCE ON TENTH GRADE BOYS (Ann Arbor, Mich.: Institute for Social Research, 1970); Epps, E. G., FAMILY AND ACHIEVEMENT: A STUDY

OF THE RELATIONS OF FAMILY BACKGROUND TO ACHIEVEMENT ORIENTATION AND PERFORMANCE AMONG URBAN NEGRO HIGH SCHOOL STUDENTS, Ann Arbor, Mich.: Institute for Social Research, 1969); Fitts, W. H., TENNESSEE SELF CONCEPT SCALE: MANUAL (Nashville: Counselor Records and Tests, 1965); Williams, R. L. and Cole, S., "Self-concept and school adjustment," PERSONNEL AND GUIDANCE JOURNAL, (46): 478-481, 1968.

7. Feldhusen, J. F., Thurston, J. R. and Benning, J. J., "Classroom behavior, intelligence and achievement," JOURNAL OF EXPERIMENTAL EDUCATION (36): 82-87, 1967; Swift, M., and Spivack, G., "The assessment of achievement-related classroom behavior," JOURNAL OF SPECIAL EDUCATION (2): 137-153, 1968.

8. Weinberg, C., "Achievement and school attitudes of adolescent boys as related to behavior and occupational status of families," SOCIAL FORCES (42): 362-466, 1964.

9. Farrington, D. P., and West, D. J., "A comparison between early delinquents and young aggressives," BRITISH JOURNAL OF CRIMINOLOGY, (11): 341-358, 1971.

10. Gold, M. and Mann, D., *supra* note 2; Mann, D., WHEN DELINQUENCY IS DEFENSIVE: SELF-ESTEEM AND DELINQUENT BEHAVIOR (Ann Arbor, Mich.: University of Michigan, 1976); Massimo, J. and Shore, M., "The effectiveness of a comprehensive, vocationally oriented psychotherapeutic program for adolescent delinquent boys," AMERICAN JOURNAL OF ORTHOPSYCHIATRY, (33): 634-642, 1963; Shore, M. F., and Massimo, J. L., "Comprehensive vocationally oriented psychotherapy for adolescent delinquent boys: a follow-up study," AMERICAN JOURNAL OF ORTHOPSYCHIATRY, (36): 609-615, 1966.

11. Kaplan, H. B., "Self-attitudes and deviant response," SOCIAL FORCES, (54): 788-801, 1976.

12. Entwistle, N. J., and Cunningham, S., "Neuroticism and school attainment – a linear relationship?" BRITISH JOURNAL OF EDUCATIONAL PSYCHOLOGY, (38): 123-132, 1968; Feldhusen, J. F., Denny, T., and Condon, C. F., "Anxiety, divergent thinking, and achievement," JOURNAL OF EDUCATIONAL PSYCHOLOGY (56): 40-45, 1965; Hundleby, J. D., "The trait of anxiety as defined by objective performance measures and indices of emotional disturbance in middle childhood,"MULTIVARIATE BEHAVIORAL RESEARCH (Special Issue): 7 - 14, 1968; Sarason, S. B., Davidson, K. S., Lighthall, F. F., Waite, R. R., and Ruebush, B. K., ANXIETY IN ELEMENTARY SCHOOL CHILDREN (New York: Wiley, 1960).

13. Douglas, J. W. B., and Ross, J. M., "Adjustment and educational progress," BRITISH JOURNAL OF CHILD PSYCHOLOGY, (38): 2-4, 1968.

14. Davies, J. G. V., and Maliphant, R., "Autonomic responses of male adolescents exhibiting refractory behavior in school," JOURNAL OF CHILD PSYCHOLOGY AND PSYCHIATRY, (12): 115-127, 1971; Laycock, A. L., "Vascular change under stress in delinquents and controls," BRITISH JOURNAL OF CRIMINOLOGY, (8): 64-69, 1968; Naar, R., "An attempt to differentiate delinquents from non-delinquents on the basis of projective drawings," JOURNAL OF CRIMINAL LAW, CRIMINOLOGY, AND POLICE SCIENCE, (55): 107–110, 1964; Shore, M. F., and Massimo, J. L., 1966, *supra* Note 10; Shore, M. F., Massimo, J. L., Mack, R., and Malasky, C., "Studies of psychotherapeutic change in adolescent delinquent boys: the role of guilt," PSYCHOTHERAPY: THEORY, RESEARCH AND PRACTICE, (5): 85-88, 1968.

15. Swidler, A., "What free schools teach," SOCIAL PROBLEMS, (24): 214-227, 1976, p. 220.

16. Bowman, P. H., "Effects of a revised school program on potential delinquents," ANNALS OF THE AMERICAN ACADEMY OF POLITICAL AND SOCIAL SCIENCE, (322): 53-62, 1959.

17. Persons, R. H., and Pepinsky, H. B., "Convergence in psychotherapy with delinquent boys," JOURNAL OF COUNSELING PSYCHOLOGY, (13): 329-334, 1966.
18. Persons, R. W., "The relationship between psychotherapy with institutionalized boys and subsequent community adjustment," JOURNAL OF CONSULTING PSYCHOLOGY, (31): 137-141, 1967.

AESTHETIC FACTORS IN SCHOOL VANDALISM

Vernon L. Allen and David B. Greenberger
University of Wisconsin

Abundant anecdotal evidence suggests that one important factor in vandalism is the sheer enjoyment experienced by vandals during destruction of an object — a factor that is generally overlooked. Perusal of case reports reveals many instances in which youngsters, in discussing their acts of vandalism, have offered unsolicited observations indicating that the destruction was, in their own words, simply "fun." Recognizing the positive emotional affect that vandals seem to obtain from their acts, some investigators have called vandalism "wreckreation." Yet the assertion that destruction is enjoyable by no means ends our inquiry into the causes of vandalism; it is only a beginning. An answer must be sought to a more fundamental question: Why is destruction so often a pleasant experience?

One explanation for the pleasure that a person derives from vandalism is that destruction is an aesthetic experience. Artists as well as psychologists have noted a close affinity between art and destruction or, more generally, between creative and destructive acts. The paradox here is more apparent than real. In construction and in destruction the novel transformation of material activates the same set of psychological variables which, in turn, account for the pleasurable sensations associated with such activities. Aesthetic theory, it is proposed, can help us to better understand the dynamics of vandalism and to design more effective preventive measures.

AESTHETIC THEORY

Recent psychological research on aesthetics and related areas has identified several variables which appear to determine affective responses to objects. According to Berlyne the positive hedonic value (pleasure or reward) of a stimulus is determined by its potential for eliciting arousal or de-arousal (1). Both arousal and de-arousal can produce positive affect under certain conditions. A moderate increase in arousal will be experienced as pleasurable up to a point of very high arousal. Beyond this point, any further increment in arousal will be unpleasant, while a decrease in arousal will be experienced as pleasurable.

Research has shown that certain structural properties of a stimulus will increase arousal, thereby producing pleasure or enjoyment under the normal range of activation. The most important stimulus factors contributing to positive hedonic value are complexity, expectation and novelty (2). Organization and psychophysical characteristics are also important. While these variables clearly are interrelated, they can be assessed separately and each has been found to be associated with the enjoyment of aesthetic stimuli.

Studies have shown, for example, that people report greater interest in and liking for more complex stimuli and that they spend more time exploring complex patterns, whether visual or auditory, than simple ones. Expectations also influence enjoyment of an object or an action; violation of an expectation creates surprise and arousal, thus eliciting a positive affective response. Research has found that people will inspect an incongruous stimulus for a longer period of time (3) and that a moderate degree of uncertainty or surprise will arouse stronger positive affect than either very high or very low uncertainty. Novelty also has long been recognized as playing a powerful role in aesthetic experiences; research subjects reveal a rapidly diminishing level of interest, arousal, and pleasure after repeated experiences with a novel stimulus (4).

With respect to psychophysical characteristics (e.g., intensity, size, and color), enjoyment tends to increase with growing intensity and size up to a point and then to decrease; and some colors (e.g., blue) commonly are preferred over others. Also, aesthetic reactions to an object are strongly influenced by factors such as organization (patterning or grouping), proportion, and symmetry. The applicability of each of these factors to any particular instance of vandalism will depend, of course, upon the qualities of the object being destroyed.

Three phases or stages of vandalism can be identified: before, during, and after destruction. In some cases, information from only one sense modality (e.g., visual) will predominate at one of the three stages. In other cases two or more senses may be involved (e.g., visual, auditory, and tactual-kinesthetic). In the first stage (before destruction) variation in appearance may exist in terms of structural variables (such as complexity, novelty, and expectedness), psychophysical properties (size or intensity), and organization (patterning) of stimulus elements. These properties determine whether an object will be judged as interesting or dull, pleasing or displeasing, beautiful or ugly. If a person expects that altering the appearance of an object will make it more interesting or pleasing, an effort may be made to change its appearance even if it means resorting to socially disapproved methods such as vandalism.

In the second phase (during an act of destruction) enjoyment derives primarily from the visual, auditory, and tactual-kinesthetic stimuli which arise during rapid transformation of an object. Because this phase involves the actual transformation of the object, the enjoyment should be most vivid here. Since the variables of size, complexity, expectedness, etc. will determine whether the process of destruction will be perceived as more or less pleasurable, the type of vandalism or destruction that will result in the greatest enjoyment can be predicted. Greater enjoyment should be derived from destroying an object if the process of breakage is, for example, more complex, more unexpected, or more novel. Objects in the environment which appear likely to break in ways that are complex, unexpected, or novel, therefore, will be sought out as objects of vandalism.

In the third phase (after destruction) the appearance of the stimulus object also can be described according to the variables specified in aesthetic theory. The static appearance of the object after destruction, for example, may be very interesting or pleasing. The patterning and organization of the object also importantly determine its post-destruction appearance. For instance, breaking particular panes of glass in a large window might leave a more interesting and pleasing pattern.

The appearance of an object and its anticipated manner of breaking may serve either as an eliciting cue (which actually evokes or stimulates acts of vandalism) or as a discriminative cue (which simply influences selection among potential targets). Even if vandalism is engaged in initially for reasons other than enjoyment (e.g., by imitation, accident, or revenge), these aesthetic variables produce positive affective reactions which will reinforce the destructive act and increase the likelihood of vandalism occurring in the future.

RESEARCH ON AESTHETICS IN VANDALISM

To test the aesthetic theory of vandalism a series of studies was undertaken involving laboratory experiments, archival data, and personal interviews. Seven laboratory experiments examined (1) various aspects of the relationship between complexity before, during, and after destruction and the inclination to damage or destroy an object; (2) the relation between expectation and enjoyment of destruction; and (3) the effects of material type and organizational factors on selection for destruction. Archival data were used in examining all incidents of vandalism in Madison, Wisconsin public schools. And, finally, personal interviews were employed to obtain firsthand information about the motivations for and experiences of destructive acts. All of these studies lend support to the aesthetic theory of vandalism.

EXPERIMENT 1: COMPLEXITY AND BEHAVIOR

It was hypothesized that the desire to destroy an object would be related to the complexity manifested in the process of its destruction as well as the complexity of the outcome (i.e., its appearance after destruction). To test this hypothesis, a silent color film was constructed showing 26 panes of glass being broken in a standardized way. To obtain a subjective scaling of complexity, 20 judges were asked to observe the film and record on a bipolar scale their judgments of the degree of complexity represented by each instance of breaking glass. After the scaling, a series of five episodes, selected to maximize the range of judges' responses, was drawn from the original 26 episodes.

The subjects (21 male and 21 female college students) observed the film and indicated how much they would like to break each piece of glass. It was found that, as hypothesized, the rank order of commitment to break a pane of glass was related directly to its rank on subjective complexity. Interestingly, there was no difference between males and females in preference. The rankings were ordered significantly in the predicted direction (p < .001), thus providing strong support for the theory.

EXPERIMENT 2: PLEASINGNESS AND INTERESTINGNESS

A second experiment was undertaken to investigate the relation between stimulus complexity and two important aspects of the hedonic value of a stimulus— pleasingness and interestingness.

On the basis of past research it was hypothesized that within a moderate range of complexity ratings of both pleasingness and interestingness would increase as the level of stimulus complexity increased. The film showing five panes of glass being broken was presented to 29 subjects. Results indicated that both pleasingness and interestingness increased with greater stimulus complexity (p < .001).

Comparing the results of the second experiment with those of the first, it was found that the curve depicting the relation between a person's desire to break an object and its complexity is similar to the relation between the pleasingness of an object and its complexity. This suggests a direct relation between a person's desire to break an object and the extent to which he finds the act pleasing — in other words, he will prefer to destroy panes of glass that break in a pleasurable way.

EXPERIMENT 3: PROCESS VERSUS OUTCOME

A third experiment examined the relative contribution of the process of destruction and of an object's appearance after destruction to judgments of complexity.

The mean ratings by 20 subjects for complexity of the process alone were almost identical to the ratings obtained for overall complexity of the sequence; but ratings for the end result differed from ratings for the overall sequence and for process. The rank-order for process complexity was identical to the rank-order for pleasingness (experiment 2) and for desire to destroy (experiment 1). The rank-order for complexity of end result was identical to ratings of interestingness (experiment 2). Thus, in rating overall complexity in the first experiment, subjects apparently gave more weight to the process of breaking than to the final result.

Considering the findings of the first three experiments together, it can be concluded that there is a strong and direct relation between the desire to destroy an object and its level of complexity during the process of breaking.

EXPERIMENT 4: EXPECTATION AND UNCERTAINTY

The fourth experiment investigated the effects of expectation or uncertainty. According to aesthetic theory, an act of destruction should be most enjoyable when it violates an established expectation. This prediction was tested by creating an experimental condition in which one of a series of episodes of breaking glass did not occur in the way that the subject had been led to expect by previous experience.

Two films consisting of four segments of glass breaking were constructed. In the first three segments of both films the glass broke the first time it was hit. In one version of the film (control condition), the glass in the fourth segment was shown breaking when hit just as it had in the first three segments; but in the other version (experimental condition), the glass in the fourth segment did not break when hit the first two times — it finally shattered on the third attempt.

After reviewing each segment of film 37 subjects indicated their degree of enjoyment. The mean score for enjoyment was significantly higher ($p < .01$) in the experimental than in the control condition on the critical segment of the film. Thus, when an expectation was violated, the experience was reported by subjects as being more enjoyable than when their expectation was confirmed.

EXPERIMENT 5: INITIAL COMPLEXITY

To investigate the role of initial complexity in selection of targets for destruction, a series of model buildings was constructed (5). Each model was a simple tower built with wooden blocks. Initial complexity was operationally defined in three ways: (1) tall versus short buildings,with the size of blocks and shape of the construction, with height, size of blocks, and shape of buildings held constant; and (3) irregular versus regular design with size of blocks and height of building held constant.

It was predicted that subjects would prefer to destroy a model with a complex as opposed to one with a simple initial structure. For each of the three pairs the 24 subjects were asked to choose which one of the two buildings they would like "to knock down — to demolish by kicking it down with your foot."

Results showed that overall 82 percent of the subjects chose the complex structure. (Males and females did not differ.) Subjects preferred the tall to the short building ($p < .001$), the building constructed of small rather than large blocks ($p < .001$), and the irregular instead of the regular design ($p < .005$).

EXPERIMENT 6: INITIAL PATTERN

It was hypothesized that an individual will choose to destroy those particular elements of an object that produce the most pleasing pattern after destruction. More specifically, choice in breaking a specific part of a window containing several panes will be determined by the pleasingness of the resulting pattern of intact and broken parts.

In order to make predictions, the aesthetic value of a large number of potential patterns had to be assessed. This was accomplished by obtaining ratings of pleasingness for 72 different patterns consisting of nine adjacent white and black squares. From these aesthetic values, it is possible to predict destruction when an act permits the creation of a variety of patterns.

A window was constructed that had the same structure as the abstract patterns used in the scaling. According to the scaling data, three black squares across the diagonal create a highly pleasing pattern. Thus, the two panes at the end of the diagonal were removed from the window, and subjects were asked to select any one of the seven unbroken panes of glass for destruction. The probability of choosing the predicted (middle) pane by chance was one in seven(14%),yet the obtained frequency for choice of the middle pane was 63 percent (17 of 27 subjects) (6). After making their initial choice, each subject was asked which of the remaining six panes he would most like to have broken. Again, as predicted, subjects chose to break a pane that resulted in the most pleasing pattern which could be created.

EXPERIMENT 7: TYPE OF MATERIAL

To test the effects of type of material on desire to destroy an object, 25 subjects were shown a film containing 19 segments of glass breaking: 13 regular window panes, four wire-safety panes (containing wire mesh), and two laminated panes (two pieces of glass with vinyl between them). After seeing each segment being broken, subjects indicated how much they would like to break such a piece of glass themselves.

For two of the three types of material — the regular window pane and the wire-safety glass — the rank order for desire to break was almost identical to the rank order for complexity. In the case of the laminated glass, however, the rank order for desire to break was substantially higher than its rank order for complexity. From the appearance of the laminated glass (it looked like regular glass panes), subjects probably expected that it would break in the same way as the regular window glass — but it did not. Subjects thus expressed a preference for the type of glass that broke in an unexpected way.

INTERVIEW DATA: INCIDENTS OF DESTRUCTION

Two additional investigations of aesthetic factors in vandalism are being undertaken in more natural settings. Open-ended personal interviews are being conducted with a sample of young males 18 to 20 years of age. We are also analyzing archival data on vandalism in the Madison, Wisconsin, public schools. Both of these approaches have already produced some support for the aesthetic theory of vandalism.

Each respondent in the interview study was asked to relate in detail all incidents in which he had broken or destroyed something (7). The respondent was asked to recall incidents in which he had deliberately broken or destroyed something, and to respond to detailed and probing questions about the three incidents involving the most extensive damage. Answers to the following questions were sought: What was the motivation for destroying the object? How did the respondent feel before, during, and after the act? Did he remember how the object looked before, during, and after the breaking? How significant was the change in appearance of the object from pre- to post-destruction? Was the respondent alone or with others while breaking the object? Did he ever return to examine the object he had broken? Why was the particular object selected to be broken?

Preliminary analyses provide interesting results. Almost all respondents were able to recall and describe acts of destruction with remarkable clarity and attention to detail. They could clearly recall the appearance of the object and the general features of the surrounding environment, as well as their feelings before, during, and after the destructive act. Moreover, they could readily state why they had chosen a particular object rather than another in close proximity to it.

The enjoyment of destruction was evident from the comments of many of those interviewed. One respondent stated that he had purposely tried to create a very complicated breakage by continuing to smash an electronics part into "smaller pieces, smaller pieces, smaller pieces." The satisfaction he derived from this act could be seen in his pleasure in recalling it. Another respondent reported that the children in his community once were allowed to destroy anything in their high school just before it was scheduled to be demolished. Under the protective eyes of the police, "thousands of kids had a lot of fun." A third respondent recalled that immediately after an act of destruction he "ran off with a feeling of exhilaration." A number of respondents implied that a somewhat different motive may lie behind some destructive acts. One person felt that he had "accomplished something by the breaking." Another, who had smashed a locker in his high school, recalled having thought proudly each time he passed it for the next three years, "There's my little destruction to this brand new school."

After completing the open-ended questions about each incident of destruction, the respondent was asked to rate the incident quantitatively on several different scales. From the responses of 30 subjects, intercorrelations among the seven scales were computed for a single incident of destruction for each respondent: that act which involved the most extensive damage. The high positive correlations found for several of the scales lend support to the findings of the laboratory studies reported above and also offer some new insights. A strong positive correlation was found between degree of enjoyment of the process of destruction and the complexity of the object while it was breaking ($r = .51$, $p < .01$). Enjoyment of destruction also was related significantly to the amount of effort exerted ($r = .60$, $p < .01$). (Of interest, too, was the very high correlation between effort and complexity of the breaking $r = .79$, $p < .01$.) A significant correlation was obtained between enjoyment and ratings of the beauty of the destruction ($r = .42$, $p < .05$), indicating that these respondents perceived an association between the aesthetic quality of an act of destruction and their enjoyment of it. Finally, as was predicted (and consistent with earlier experimental findings), interestingness was highly correlated with enjoyment ($r = .64$, $p < .01$).

INCIDENTS OF SCHOOL VANDALISM

A study of vandalism in the public schools of Madison, Wisconsin, that has occurred during the past five years is currently underway. It is hoped that with data from this study it will be possible to determine if certain objects are selected to be vandalized because of their stimulus characteristics, as predicted by aesthetic theory. Each act of vandalism is being coded to indicate type of damage, size and visibility of object, proximity to street and lighting, nearness to projectiles, type of room, time of year, weather, etc. When all items have been coded in detail the data will be analyzed to uncover any general consistencies and associations among variables. While it is too early to draw any firm conclusions from the data, it is already clear that certain types of objects are vandalized more frequently than others and some items are vandalized repeatedly in particular schools.

IMPLICATIONS FOR RESEARCH AND ACTION

A number of important areas for further research on the aesthetics of vandalism can be identified. First, research is needed on the roles of the various sense modalities and their interaction. The empirical studies reported here have dealt only with one sense modality — vision. Yet, according to anecdotal accounts, auditory cues may be much more important than visual cues in many cases of vandalism. Tactual-kinesthetic information is particularly important in destruction involving direct contact with the object (e.g., kicking or striking), as opposed to contact at a distance (e.g., throwing a rock). Expectations concerning the feedback and resistance accompanying the act also may influence affective reactions. Research is needed to assess the relative importance of auditory, visual, and tactual-kinesthetic cues in different types of vandalism.

Second, there are many important questions involving motivation and arousal. Research is needed to investigate the contribution of frustration, anger, boredom, and other sources of arousal to the positive aesthetic experience obtained from an act of destruction. For example, how does anger or frustration affect the relationship between aesthetic variables and the experience of enjoyment? The two-factor theory of aesthetics advanced by Berlyne (8) offers some hints, but more research will be necessary to fully answer these questions.

Third, research should be conducted on the relation between aesthetic theory and the self. Can destruction be considered an aesthetic response in the sense that it is one way of altering (and thereby controlling) a portion of the environment? If so, is destruction simply another form of self-expression as has been suggested with regard to the phenomenon of graffiti (9)? What is the relation between characteristics of the self (e.g., control, esteem, and aesthetic needs) and the hedonic value of vandalism? Are objects that are beautiful less likely to be vandalized and, if so, why?

Finally, aesthetic theory can be applied to a much wider range of acts of vandalism than those discussed here. It is interesting to note, for example, that fire has all the stimulus characteristics that would insure a very high hedonic value. Vandalism by fire does occur in the schools. Research on arson from the point of view of aesthetic theory might shed a great deal of light on this form of vandalism.

In the meantime, enough is already known about the aesthetics of vandalism to offer some guidance concerning

61

prevention. According to aesthetic theory, vandalism could be greatly reduced simply by making it a less enjoyable experience. Vandalism can be made less enjoyable by selecting structures, designs, and types of material which minimize complexity, unexpectedness, and novelty while reducing the temptation to "improve" the appearance of an object or its environment by defacement or destruction.

Various materials differ widely in appearance and sounds they produce during destruction. Architects have noted that glass, composite materials, asbestos, and tile hangings are highly susceptible to attack (10). One way of reducing the enjoyment and interestingness of breaking glass is to substitute plastic. Using subjective scaling techniques, it would be easy to assess the affective value associated with destruction of a wide range of materials. Based on such scaling results, types could be selected which are less enjoyable to break, and these could be used in locations that are highly susceptible to vandalism.

Any object which can be made more aesthetically pleasing by creating a particular organization through destruction is a candidate for vandalism. Enjoyment of vandalism can be reduced by avoiding patterns that encourage attack. A window with a large center pane surrounded by smaller panes, for example, often looks more balanced after breaking the center pane than before. Windows also should be constructed in small units, since a small window generally breaks in a simpler and less interesting way, and with less noise, than a larger one.

Other recommendations for reducing vandalism can be drawn from aesthetic theory. Damage by vandalism should be repaired immediately to deprive the perpetrators of the opportunity to admire their handiwork. At night, lighting should be directed away from windows to prevent vandals from seeing the process of destruction or its outcome. Socially approved ways of altering the school environment should be offered to students (e.g., "scribbling walls" or graffiti boards) as an alternative to disapproved destruction. A short course could be developed to present psychological theories of aesthetics through audio-visual materials, exposition of theory, and empirical studies. Art classes could adopt a broader definition of aesthetics to encompass both constructive and destructive acts.

Finally, and perhaps most important, students should be made aware of the psychological processes contributing to their enjoyment of destruction. Reasons for the enjoyment of vandalism should be identified and fully discussed. The problem of school vandalism may be most effectively controlled by giving students a better understanding of the psychological basis of such behavior, and by encouraging them to express their aesthetic tendencies in equally satisfying but less damaging ways.

FOOTNOTES

1. Berlyne, D. E. AESTHETICS AND PSYCHOBIOLOGY (New York: Appleton-Century-Crofts, 1971).
2. *Ibid.*
3. Nunnally, J. C., Faw, T. T., and Bashford, M. B., "The effect of degrees incongruity on visual fixations in children and adults," JOURNAL OF EXPERIMENTAL PSYCHOLOGY, 81, 360-364, 1969.
4. Berlyne, D. E., and Parham, L. C., "Determinants of subjective novelty," PERCEPTION AND PSYCHOPHYSICS, 3, 415-423, 1968.
5. This experiment was conducted in collaboration with Daniel R. Spencer.
6. This is significantly higher than the expected frequency of $X^2 (6) = 48.30, p < .001$.
7. This study was supported by the Institute for Research on Poverty, University of Wisconsin.
8. *Op. cit. supra* note 1.
9. Kurlansky, M., Noar, J., and Mailer, N., THE FAITH OF

GRAFFITI (New York: Alskog/Praeger, 1974).

10. Leather, A., and Matthews, A., "What the architect can do: a series of design guides," in C. Ward (ed.), VANDALISM (New York: Van Nostrand Reinhard, 1973), pp. 117-172.

THE OBSOLESCENCE OF ADOLESCENCE

Jack Hruska
School of Education
University of Massachusetts

Technology and urbanization have significantly changed twentieth-century America and one of the more dramatic changes has been in the role of youth. Society no longer needs them. Their productive energies have been replaced in the home by processed food and natural gas; in the labor market by machines, computers, and adults. And, since social relationships are heavily influenced by the production system, for young people these too have been severely circumscribed.

As adolescents move toward physical and intellectual maturity, they have intense needs for meaningful work and social activities. Yet, during this 13- to 19-year old period they are confined to the role of student, which is, essentially, no more than preparation for taking an active part in society at some future time. The role of student is meaningful only to some — perhaps a minority, while to many it is unbearably limiting and frustrating. Those who are unable to satisfy themselves with preparing to live feel useless, alienated, cut off from many of their peers and from the society which can find for them no alternative to attending school. Frequently, the response of these outcast youth is to wreak havoc on that society, and especially on those social institutions which most directly and personally reject or frustrate them. School crime is one result. There are others — drug abuse, delinquency, youthful rebellion and suicide.

The problem of school crime, therefore, is not so much a school problem as it is a cultural problem manifested in schools. Cultural changes in the family, in work environments, and in

65

the community have eroded the developmental significance for youth of social institutions other than school. As extended families have been replaced by nuclear families, the number and variety of people with whom adolescents closely interact has been systematically reduced. Not only are there fewer grandparents, aunts and uncles, cousins and siblings, but there are fewer opportunities and less time for intimate or productive involvements.

The community and the work setting also have changed. Communities no longer are characterized by small farms, small businesses, and people who know each other, suffer together, celebrate together, hate and love together. Rather, they are places of systematic segregation: families in residential areas; workers in offices or in plants; doctors in medical centers; shopkeepers in the mall; the old in nursing homes, and the young in school. While it is difficult to fault the legislation that freed children from hard labor in the mines and the mills, compulsory schooling, coupled with other changes in the work environment, has excluded children and adolescents from close involvement with work and workers. And, to the degree that it is productive and meaningful, work has been a primary source of identity and social interaction throughout recorded history.

One of the most obvious consequences of the evolution of family, work, and community, then, has been the steady erosion of the role of youth. In each case, opportunities for purposeful activity, for meaningful interaction with adults, and for the testing of competencies under "real-life" conditions have been reduced as our culture has further postponed the age at which such opportunities become available. Virtually the only arena in which today's adolescents have a socially recognized and accepted role is in the secondary school (1); yet this institution never was intended, nor is it equipped, to meet all of the varied needs of children and youth.

LIMITATIONS OF SECONDARY SCHOOLING

Cultural developments over the past century have culminated in a shift in responsibility for adolescent development from the family and community institutions to the secondary school. In 1900, six percent of all eligible youth graduated from high school; today that figure is over 90 percent. As the length of secondary schooling has increased, so have our expectations. Schools which were once concerned primarily with the three R's now are asked to take on many responsibilities and tasks that formerly belonged to the family, the community, and the employer. At present, the secondary schools are beleaguered with Humanistic Education, Special Education, Sex Education, Career Education, Environmental Education, Open Education, Vocational Education, Consumer Education, Health Education, and Value Clarification — and it has become clear that they cannot fulfill such multiple and frequently contradictory expectations.

The Achilles heel of secondary curriculum structure is that while it is a rational and logical organization of knowledge, it has been pushed far beyond its psychological limits. The passivity required of secondary school students runs counter to the adolescent need for activity. Anyone familiar with junior and senior high schools knows how difficult it can be to control the physical energy of students. Yet, secondary schools must repress not only the physical movement of students but their psychological tendencies as well. That is, whereas an adolescent tends to live fully in the present, the secondary school curriculum focuses almost exclusively on preparing young people for the future. Whereas adolescents feel the need to experiment with new ways of interacting with their environment, the process of schooling denies them the opportunity to do so.

Rather than providing real experiences, the secondary school curriculum simply transmits society's accumulated experiences. Students are not asked to rediscover principles and theories or to undergo the varied human experiences and feelings. These experiences, instead, are boiled down into formulae, short stories, lectures, and readings, injected into lessons and courses, and organized into a curriculum. Schools are structured so that students "move through" the courses and "cover" the material so they can somehow "learn" to lead more rational, meaningful, and useful lives. This rational breakdown of the world into compartmentalized disciplines, and the refinement of those disciplines into sub-units which are further divided into micro-units, leaves the motivation to learn entirely to the student. Unfortunately, only a portion of our adolescents can identify with that academic approach to the world and the grading and ranking procedures of the schools allow only about half of all students to succeed.

THE PREPARATION TRAP

At the heart of the problem of our secondary schools lies the notion that adolescence should be devoted wholly to preparation for later life. Since society has no economic or social need for adolescents, this period of life has been designated for academic or vocational preparation. This was not, of course, the result of a thoughtful decision grounded in adolescent psychology, but merely an extension of the conventional wisdom that education is a good thing – the more of it the better – and that more education can be equated with more schooling.

The idea that these formative years should be given over to preparation for later life has numerous psychological ramifications. Even a cursory examination of adolescence should make anyone skeptical that such a volatile period of growth could be contained by years of preparation for vaguely defined future tasks. In 1938 John Dewey wrote:

> . . . Now 'preparation' is a treacherous idea. In a certain sense every experience should do something to prepare a person for later experiences of a deeper and more expansive quality. That is the very meaning of growth, continuity, reconstruction of experience. But it is a mistake to suppose that the mere acquisition of a certain amount of arithmetic, geography, history, etc., which is taught and studied because it may be useful at some time in the future, has this effect, and it is a mistake to suppose that acquisition

of skills in reading and figuring will automatically constitute preparation for their right and effective use under conditions very unlike those in which they were acquired (2).

Looking back, the contemporary problems of secondary schools were predictable. Schools were most successful when they did not have to succeed — when there were educational alternatives such as apprenticeships in farm and factory work, when there were others means of social and economic advancement, and when a lifestyle without school was a viable alternative for adolescents. If the "preparatory" curriculum of earlier times became too stultifying, a youngster could leave the school and join the community in another role. Today, however, in the absence of alternative community roles, those young people who, in any former era, would have left school remain under protest, expending much of their energy in maintaining a youth culture aimed at meeting the psychological needs ignored by the adult culture. This youth culture, which is largely unassisted by adults but thoroughly exploited by the mass media, has become a powerful influence on adolescents.

In short, adolescent misbehavior is largely a product of their systematic isolation from the community; of their subjection to preparatory schooling that provides only limited psychological rewards; and of the formation of a youth subculture that is, at best, superficial. It should come as no surprise that our youth are disposed to apathy, cynicism, irresponsibility, and violence to themselves and others. They have been disinherited and their behavior patterns are those of disinherited peoples everywhere.

A notable characteristic of contemporary youth culture is its contradictions: the idealism and the cynicism, the rejection of authority and the emulation of idols, the striving for individuation and the rigid loyalty to peers, the abundance of energy in some situations and the lethargy and apathy of others. Exuberant gaiety, laughter, and euphoria give way to depressive gloom and melancholy. Much of this behavior probably can be attributed to the loss of identity which has accompanied the erosion of meaningful adolescent roles. Not knowing who they are or who they are becoming, adolescents exhibit seemingly incongruous behavior in search of clarity and meaning. They lash out in frustration and anger, often randomly, at the society which has disowned them.

They do not live up to our expectations, to be sure; but, if one posits a reasonable — or at least neutral — benevolence toward human nature, fault can be found with society more than with the young. That is, if we assume that, given equal opportunity, young people would rather be a part of the dominant culture, economically and socially productive, accepted by their neighbors, creative rather than destructive, and sound of body and mind, then we must assume that somehow their opportunities to choose those alternatives have been blocked. The only lasting solution to the fundamental cultural problem of our disinherited young lies, it seems, in the creation for them of alternative or complementary roles outside the traditional school or work setting.

DIRECTIONS FOR CHANGE

Perhaps the single greatest impediment to change in the lifestyles of adolescents are the common assumptions which exclude potential solutions. The problem too often is viewed as one of finding the proper relationship between school and work, or preparation for work. Young people are expected to go to school either to prepare for more schooling or to prepare for a job. Secondary education, as a result, has been polarized into academic and vocational education, which only thinly disguises the fact that even the academic program is designed to pave the way to a better job.

In spite of this tenacious notion that the only acceptable options for young adults are schooling or a part-time job, there is mounting evidence that these two alternatives are no longer sufficient. Many now argue that the solution lies in some combination of the two (e.g., cooperative education), as if alternating two programs lacking a certain desirable quality will somehow make up for that lack. Yet, especially in view of the critical shortage of jobs represented by our 7.5 percent unemployment rate, it seems that we must jettison the entrenched belief that school, a job, or some combination thereof represent the only possible settings for adolescent development.

A key to the solution proposed here lies in the distinction between work and jobs. Work is a broader term, more pregnant with meaning, than the word "job." Purposeful work requires the exercise of insight, intelligence, judgment, and style. Work is done to accomplish some goal and for the feeling of success, self-worth or wholeness it brings. It requires that the worker have some control over his working conditions and the quality of his product and that he have a predisposition to engage in the particular activity. When work is done solely for economic return, we call it a job.

Abraham Maslow, the psychologist who developed the concept of a "hierarchy of needs," repeatedly stressed the importance of significant work for human fulfillment. He wrote:

> . . . This business of self-actualization via a commitment to an important job and to worthwhile work could also be said, then, to be the path of human happiness . . . The other way — of seeking for personal salvation — just doesn't work for anybody I have ever seen . . . The only happy people I know are the ones who are working well at something they consider important (3).

Yet most of the things people do to earn money are in fact jobs. With the advent of Taylor's time-and-motion studies 50 years ago, our economic practice has been to make work structures a function of, and subordinate to, the production of material goods. The resulting subdivision of work into isolated repetitive functions, easily learned and requiring little intelligence or creativity, has transformed work into labor, eliminating careers and creating jobs. The lack of meaningful work was a cornerstone of Paul Goodman's book, GROWING

UP ABSURD, in which he points out that our society is "lacking in enough man's work:"

> . . . there get to be fewer jobs that are necessary or unques-
> tionably useful; that require energy and draw on some of
> one's best capacities; and that can be done keeping one's
> honor and dignity (4).

It is clear that neither schooling nor the jobs available to young people provide the kinds of environments or activities needed for healthy adolescent development. A better solution may lie in the creation of opportunities for youth to engage in genuine work. In order to reverse the obsolescence of adolescents we need to determine what it is that adolescents need to develop into responsible adults and how these needs can best be met with available social resources.

ALTERNATIVES FOR YOUTH

While no attempt to list the developmental needs of youth can hope to be complete, or even wholly accurate, the following is offered as a tentative step in this direction. It is suggested that the growth-producing experiences which should be made available include opportunities for young people (1) to effectively manage their own affairs (e.g., use of time, finances, choice of learning environments); (2) to interact with people of different ages; (3) to be responsible for themselves and for others; (4) to participate in group activities directed toward collective goals; (5) to create in ways that culminate in finished products; (6) to gain competencies without necessarily rooting them in preparation for a career; (7) to gain personal and direct experience with other cultures, other races, other lifestyles; and (8) to give unselfishly to others.

These eight objectives have several characteristics in common. First, they are not grounded primarily in the accumulation of more information or cognitive skills. This is because the "problem" of adolescence is believed to derive from their lack of social and economic usefulness, not from any lack in the kind of knowledge now taught in school. Second, each of these objectives has a self-knowledge component; that is, through involvement in projects with others and using varied materials youth are helped to find out what they can do and how others respond to them, thereby gaining insights into themselves. Such opportunities to develop and demonstrate competencies are essential to maturation, as Friedenberg has pointed out:

> *Respect for competence in oneself and others is crucial in adolescence, for it is crucial to self-definition. In a world as empirical as ours, a youngster who does not know what he is good at will not be sure what he is good for, he must know what he can do in order to know who he is* (5).

Another point to be made about these objectives is that they are, for the most part, already being met in private and exclusive ways for the children of the well-to-do. For generations the upper classes have provided music and dance lessons, trips abroad, summer camps, backpacking into the mountains, early introductions to the family business, cameras, power tools, allowances to be managed, elderly caretakers, and even opportunities for volunteer service for their children. It is suggested here that we come to recognize these objectives as valuable for all adolescents and provide the necessary opportunities within our overall developmental scheme.

And finally, these objectives, by and large, cannot be achieved in any significant way by expanding jobs and activities currently available in the profit-making sector. Profit-making, which is concerned with maximizing production, standardizing output, and reducing labor costs, is mostly antithetical to the principles they express. We have no reason to expect that profit-making ventures can encourage and support human interaction, creativity, experimentation, cooperation, or compassion. The notion that the problems of youth can be solved by building bridges between the school and the business community thus is rejected and attention is turned to as yet untapped sources of growth-production experiences for youth (6).

73

SOME PROGRAM EXAMPLES

The following twelve programs or projects are offered as examples of the kinds of activity likely to promote achievement of the developmental objectives listed above. Their organization and administration, of course, would vary as a function of local conditions.

1. *Ecological Projects.* Every city, town, and crossroads has felt the impact of commercialism run amuck. We need not elaborate on the fact that countless rivers, parks, fields, woods, ponds, and mountains are in need of cleansing.

2. *Aesthetic Projects.* Similarly, we have badly neglected the opportunity to beautify our nation as we wantonly harvested its resources. Virtually every community in America could lift the spirits of its citizens if our young people were put to work applying paints, peonies, and picket fences to the premises.

3. *Cultural Events.* A group of students might take six months off to produce two or three plays. They could make the props, play the parts, and even write the scripts. The same idea could be applied to music, dance, flower shows, and art. Local radio and TV are equally adaptable to the purposes of generating a public audience.

4. *News Reporting.* What town would not gain by having a TV, radio, or newspaper operated by a group of local youth? The intent, of course, would not be to compete with commercial producers, but to augment them by offering another perspective.

5. *Inventing Projects.* Laboratories could be set up to enable inquisitive young scientists to experiment with ideas of interest to them.

6. *Human Services.* Through systematic segmentation we have placed artificial barriers between people who are much in need of one another. Elderly people need the young, the very

young need the adolescents, and the ill and depressed need the healthy and the spirited. Compassionate and thoughtful people could readily devise schemes for bringing these groups together for extended periods of time.

7. *Arts and Crafts.* We need only to provide space, materials, and legitimacy to get adolescents to spend endless hours working (in the best sense of the word) with wood, metals, leather, plastics, and many other products that have enticed the creative spirit in people throughout recorded history.

8. *Construction.* There is much need for building projects which are not delivered by the profit of economy. The young need playgrounds, the elderly need rooms remodeled and almost everyone needs a tool shed. What better mixture of people and materials can there be when a crew of girls and boys help an elderly couple turn an attic into a greenhouse?

9. *Skill Development.* Adolescents crave mastery and 15 or 16 year olds might well spend their time learning electronics, stereo repair, carpentry, cooking, cattle-raising, or photography. Such skill-oriented programs should be directed toward the growth and development of youth, attending as much to social, spiritual, and aesthetic needs as to technical skill development.

10. *Academic Sabbatical.* One of the joys of the academic profession is the sabbatical, a "moratorium" designed to enable and even encourage people to lose themselves in a self-selected project. The concept could be readily extended to young scholars who might want to spend several months studying black history, feminism, sail-boating, astronomy, or another topic of particular interest to them.

11. *Travel.* The potential for enabling young people to spend several months in other towns, states, and countries is virtually unlimited. Why should the "year abroad" be restricted to the independently wealthy?

12. *Business.* Models already exist throughout the country

75

in which young people organize, set up, and operate a business. This seems, intuitively, to offer the kinds of experiences needed by those youths who now spend incalculable amounts of time and energy "ripping off" someone else's business.

These twelve ideas have been selected somewhat arbitrarily. The list could easily be quadrupled in a matter of minutes. Once we extend our thinking beyond formal schooling and part-time jobs as the only appropriate alternatives for youth we are inundated by a host of creative opportunities. Unfortunately, almost any competent school board member or school adminis-trator could give five good reasons why each of these twelve ideas is "inoperable" — parental resistance, lack of funds, federal and state laws, unions, student immaturity, college requirements, and so on. In 1960, the same people had five good reasons why we could never get to the moon. The difficul-ties inherent in instituting sabbaticals for 15-year olds should not be underestimated; but prolonged adolescence is a social invention, not a physiological fact, and social institutions can be altered. Problems certainly will arise over the issues of money, time, school, the private sector, and other institutions, so perhaps a word on each may be in order.

Funds. Obtaining public funds for education is difficult and getting more so, but, as Paul Goodman pointed out years ago, these kinds of projects could easily be funded for the same amount of money now spent to keep these youngsters in school. Given the high costs of vandalism it is absurd to suggest that we cannot afford programs for youth.

Time. Many of the ideas suggested are already available in the public schools, yet these do not serve the same ends. There is a vast difference between spending eight hours a day for six months in a metal craftshop working with other craftspeople of different ages and sexes and attending metal-shop in a public school for forty-seven minutes each day with one's peers.

School. The regular school, of course, would go on as before. These alternative "sabbatical" projects would be available and students would move in and out of them as they seek an appropriate balance of academics, jobs, and alternative experiences. These alternatives are not meant to demean academic education; on the contrary, they are intended to enrich it, deepen it, broaden it, and make it available to more students for longer periods of time.

The Private Sector. Many people will argue that such projects would compete with the profit-making sector of our economy and, further, that all of these objectives could be achieved in cooperation with the business community. It must be acknowledged that they would compete to some extent with business and so our already mixed economic system would become somewhat more mixed, but not awesomely so. But the objectives of a profit-seeking enterprise are so blatantly different from those of adolescent development that reconciliations probably are impossible.

Other Institutions. One of the joys of initiating these projects clearly is that they often involve interaction with an institution or group badly in need of such involvement. This mutual advantage is, of course, what makes such projects attractive. While adolescents need to act as models for younger children, younger children also need adolescent models. While adolescents need the wisdom and understanding of the aged, the aged need to feel they are giving such understanding. While adolescents need to build, refurbish, and paint, there is much that needs to be built, refurbished, and painted. In this way, all that a local educator needs to do to develop a worthwhile project is to look around the community to see how people's lives could be better and then find a way to tie that need to the energy, native intelligence, and compassion of youth. If we wish to turn the tide of wastefulness which squanders adolescent lives, then we must redesign the world in which they are asked to grow up. We lack not the wisdom but the will.

FOOTNOTES

1. This case must not be over-stated. Statistics still show that many high-school youth, perhaps as many as half, hold part-time jobs; we cannot expect the part-time work available to students to provide the growth-producing experiences they desperately need. As noted in the Special Task Force Report of the Secretary of HEW, WORK IN AMERICA, the quality of jobs in the United States is causing widespread concern among economists, industrialists, and the medical profession, particularly those involved with mental health. Since even jobs held by adults are coming to be characterized by repetition and boredom, hierarchical authority, and a lack of opportunities for creative expression or self-assertion, it seems all the more likely that the part-time jobs available to the young will be devoid of rewarding experiences.
2. Dewey, J., EXPERIENCE AND EDUCATION (New York: Collier Books, 1967), p. 47.
3. Maslow, A., EUPSYCHIAN MANAGEMENT (New York: Richard Irwin, 1968).
4. Goodman, P., GROWING UP ABSURD (New York: Vintage Books, 1968).
5. Friedenberg, E., THE VANISHING ADOLESCENT (New York: Dell, 1959).
6. For many of these ideas the author is indebted to the Panel on Youth of the President's Science Advisory Committee, chaired by James S. Coleman. Their report, YOUTH IN TRANSITION (University of Chicago Press, 1974) proposed the "establishment of alternative environments for the transition to adulthood." While they relied rather heavily on the private sector for solutions, the report is a superb statement of the problem.

SCHOOL CRIME, POWER, AND
THE STUDENT SUBCULTURE

Robert L. David
The American University

Alan Jay Lincoln
University of New Hampshire

Many critics of contemporary education have expressed a preoccupation with the school's overwhelming power over students (1). Acceptance of this notion of "student-as-victim" has led to the widespread belief, among both supporters and critics of the school system, that all power rests with the school. At the same time, those who subscribe to this notion also assume that students are not complete social beings, that they lack a collective social order or culture such as that shared by adults. While students are not viewed as wholly lacking a social order, theirs generally is defined as a student "subculture."

There is an obvious contradiction between the notion that students are only partial social beings and the belief that a student subculture does exist: the former assumes that social power is unidirectional, while the latter suggests multidirectional and multiple spheres of power. If there is a student subculture, therefore, the view of the student-as-victim can be only partially correct. Educational institutions undoubtedly wield enormous power over their students. As numerous studies have shown, the school does define and influence their present and future lives. But students, supported by their subculture, respond in ways which tend to counterbalance the power of the educational institution. Analysis of the types of power employed by students and by school personnel may help to resolve this apparent inconsistency.

BASES OF SOCIAL POWER

Social power is a complex sociological concept. Power, which can be defined as the ability to alter behavior, only rarely is distributed equally among members of a population. Typically, some participants have greater power than others; thus the ability to alter behavior (or beliefs, attitudes, and values) is not uniformly distributed.

According to French and Raven (2) there are five different types of power. Two closely related types of power are the ability to provide rewards and the ability to administer punishments. It is useful to consider these and other types of power from the viewpoint of the person being influenced. For example, if the person influenced perceives that the influencer can provide rewards (or punishments), then his responses are being influenced by reward (or coercive) power. Others, of course, may perceive the same situation in a different way. Teachers have *reward power* over most students because teachers are perceived as able to promote them or give them high grades, positive recommendations, or job leads. Other students may not recognize these as potential rewards, responding instead to the teacher's coercive power. The teacher's ability to administer punishment is clear. Teachers and school administrators not only can provide low grades, disciplinary actions, and poor recommendations, but they may initiate police proceedings, refer students to parents, and so on.

Expertise is a third basis of power. If a teacher is perceived as having special skills or knowledge, then *expert power* may be used to influence students. This type of power, which is related directly to the amount and range of expertise perceived, may be linked with reward power in the views of some students. Power may also be based upon identification. In this case — *referent power* — the relationship or imagined relationship between a student and a teacher is the basis for influence. Some teachers are able to influence some of their students because of the positive feelings these students have towards them. Students influence other students in much the same way.

The fifth type of power is *legitimate power*. Certain people or categories of people are perceived as having authority because they possess certain characteristics. Power also may derive from the position held by the individual, such as "teacher," "principal," "superintendent." In either case, legitimate power is employed when the person being influenced believes that the manipulator has the right to influence his behavior. Many students are responsive to teachers because they acknowledge the teacher's legitimate right to use power.

Teachers thus have a variety of power bases available to them. They may, in fact, be able to draw upon all five types of power, influencing some students with expert power or reward power and others with legitimate or coercive power. Some students, of course, do not respond to any attempts by teachers to influence them. These non-responsive students do not acknowledge the legitimate power of teachers and administrators, nor do they respond to any of the readily available rewards and punishments. In general, however, teachers are likely to have multiple power resources to draw on in their interactions with students.

In contrast, students typically have fewer power resources available to them in dealing with school personnel. The legitimate power associated with the position of student is not perceived as an important force. Referent power is limited; in fact, teachers are discouraged from developing personal relationships with students because of the sheer size of their classes and the complicating aspects of such relationships. The ability of students to reward teachers is severely limited, as is the teacher's recognition of student expertise. Some rewards can be provided by students who contribute to successful and enjoyable teaching; but it is clear that students have much less reward power than their teachers. Students attempting to alter the behavior of others or improve their own situation thus may resort to the use of coercive power — the only major power resource available to students. The use of coercive power, it seems, is widespread. Over 70,000 serious assaults against teachers were reported last year and property damage to schools ran to over a half billion dollars (3) — the vast majority of this violence perpetrated by students.

The use of coercive power by students occurs within and is supported by the student subculture, which is developed, over the years, in order to satisfy individual and collective needs within an institution which has disproportionate power and control. Examining the historical process by which the student subculture develops, then, may shed light on the origins of disruptive student behavior and help in the effort to design effective preventive measures.

THE STUDENT SUBCULTURE AS COUNTER-ACTION

The antisocial behaviors of students during the first three years of grade school represent not random acts, but collective and individual attempts to test the extent of the school's and the teacher's power. Since these young students lack the experience of having tested the school's authority, their subculture is unquestionably in a state of social infancy. Nevertheless, by the age of six, children generally understand that they must go to school. They also seem to sense that, since their parents cannot take them out of school without permission, they also are subject to the school's higher authority. For a child of six who has believed that his parents exercise total social power, this realization must have considerable impact upon his attempt to place the school in perspective. Out of this awareness may emerge an understanding among these young students and their peers that they are alone in confronting the institutional power of the school.

From the fourth through the seventh grades of school, the student subculture takes on a more definite form. Most students in this age group can no longer be trusted to monitor classrooms conscientiously or to inform on unruly classmates. Further examples of collective student disobedience are the exclusion of teachers from their confidence and primitive attempts to disrupt lessons by use of water guns, rubber bands, paper wads, or bean shooters. In these grades, most students still act individually to counter the school's rules and experience individual punishment for misbehavior, but there already are indicators that the student subculture is becoming more complex. Students pass notes, punish their peers by collective ostracism, and create their own language and dress styles. Increasingly violent acts also occur among this age group.

By junior and certainly senior high school, the student subculture has all the characteristics of a social structure. It has a shared history, its own language and dress styles, and a normative value structure which does not necessarily conform to that of the larger society. In high school, the separation between teachers and students is even more pronounced. Student cliques compete with each other for rewards and recognition, but they often collaborate in activities which defy the school's rules. The forms of counter-control exhibited by the student subculture frequently are so sophisticated that apprehension of guilty parties by school officials is difficult if not impossible. Student counter-control activities may include smoking on school grounds, flushing "cherry bombs" down the toilets, making anonymous bomb threats, setting off fire alarms, turning over fire extinguishers, "accidentally" spilling noxious acid, disrupting classes with untraceable noises, cheating collectively, falsifying permission slips, or expressing public contempt for the teacher's authority by means of graffiti, to name but a few. Such rowdy, mischievous, and violent student behavior constitutes a major discipline problem with which teachers and officials in many schools have long been trying to deal.

While it is difficult to assess the costs of disruptive behavior in terms of time and economic loss to the school, not to mention the students' education, just how significant the loss may be is indicated by Deutsch:

> *Most teachers would, I think, agree with me that we spend about 75 percent of our time disciplining the children and about 25 percent of our time teaching. Even the time spent in teaching is only about 10 percent effec-*

tive because of having to stop several times during a lesson to speak to certain children (4).

SCHOOL CRIME, POWER, AND FREEDOM

Student responses to powerlessness in the school setting include more serious criminal acts of violence and vandalism as well as merely disruptive classroom behavior. Vandalism, which also is routinely found among prisoners, mental patients, and workers in business and industry (5), can be viewed as another attempt by students to combat excessive institutional power. Students, like other institutionalized groups, build their own social structure that enables them collectively to resist institutional power while giving them enough freedom to engage in individual acts of aggression or destruction as well. Such a subcultural social structure not only provides students with a collective identity and alternative norms and values, but also enables them to exert some degree of control over the very institution that attempts to control them. Viewed in this light, the term "sabotage" may be more appropriate in many instances of vandalism.

Violence, too, can be seen as an attempt to counteract the superior power of a social institution. Studies of the relationship between power and conflict have shown that limitations upon personal freedom are at times related to heightened levels of conflict. The notion that deprivation of freedom facilitates conflict has been examined under varying degrees of structure or regulation in dormitories, intentional communities, monasteries, prisons, and boarding schools (6). In these structured settings, it was found that the greater the perceived deprivation of freedom, the greater the reported violence. In other settings, violence was further enhanced when anticipated levels of freedom were high (7).

While restrictions on student power and freedom in the school setting undoubtedly increase the likelihood of violence and vandalism, the school is not wholly at fault. It is, in part, the larger society which must be held accountable for the creation and persistence of the student subculture as well as for the encouragement of violence by example. Students create a subculture to meet their needs within the school setting, but they use techniques of organization and action which they see adults use in the world around them. Also, the magnitude of violence in society — at home, on the streets, in the mass media, suggests to young people that aggression is an acceptable and effective means of solving problems or settling disputes.

In part, then, school crime is modeled after behavior in the community. If students feel a need to correct the imbalance of power in the school setting, the existence of violence in the community may encourage the choice of violent modes of rebellion. Unfortunately, the school is likely to respond to increasing violence by students by relying even more heavily on institutional power to further limit students' freedom. And, in this situation, perpetuation and escalation of conflict and higher levels of violence, vandalism, and disruptive behavior — are virtually unavoidable.

Why do schools continue to pursue corrective policies that perpetuate student violence and vandalism? The principal reason is that they cannot deal effectively with the real source of the problem: the place of young people in society. Schools reflect society and they operate to reinforce the status quo. Education, despite the popular rhetoric, does not guarantee students social and economic opportunities in later life — a fact of which students apparently are not unaware. A handbook on disrupting schools, produced by a group of high school students, has this to say in its introduction:

> This pamphlet is not written for people who are not yet sure whether school is good or bad. It is written for students that realize the way that compulsory education and grades destroy the natural curiosity so many children feel, who realize how the tracking system keeps the poor people and minorities in our society on the bottom while keeping the rich and powerful on the top, who realize the danger of teaching complete obedience to authority, and

who are fed up with the racism and sexism in schools. It is written for students who have "gone through channels" trying to correct these problems and who tired of helplessly waiting while the schools destroy more and more minds each day. It is written for young people who realize that because they are trapped in school they don't have a chance to learn what they need to know to create a free and good life (8).

Students attack the school because this source of power — and perceived injustice — is at least tangible, while the legal, political, and economic system is so diffused as a focal point for rebellion that it is targeted only sporadically. The school, in effect, is caught in the middle, forced to deal with problems that, for the most part, it did not create. The best hope for reducing student crime and disruption lies in redressing, to some extent, the severe imbalance of power between youth and the social institutions which define and limit their lives, yet to date neither the school nor the larger society has taken any significant steps in this direction (9). This missing impetus for change undoubtedly will insure the continued escalation of student disruption as both the school and its student population struggle for survival.

FOOTNOTES

1. Erikson, E. CHILDHOOD AND SOCIETY, 2nd ed. (New York: Norton, 1963) and YOUTH, IDENTITY AND CRISIS (New York: Norton, 1968); Friedenberg, E., THE DIGNITY OF YOUTH AND OTHER ATAVISMS (Boston:Beacon Press,1965);Hall,S.,ADOLESCENCE: ITS PSYCHOLOGY AND ITS RELATIONS TO PHYS-IOLOGY, ANTHROPOLOGY, SOCIOLOGY, SEX,

CRIME, RELIGION AND EDUCATION (New York: D. Appleton, 1904); Henry, J. CULTURE AGAINST MAN (New York: Random House, 1963) and ON EDUCATION (New York: Random House, 1971); Keniston, K., YOUTH AND DISSENT: THE RISE OF A NEW OPPOSITION (New York: Harcourt, Brace, Jovanovich, 1971); Kohl, H., "The open classroom," NEW YORK REVIEW OF BOOKS, 1969; Kozol, J., DEATH AT AN EARLY AGE (Boston: Houghton Mifflin, 1968); Lopate, P., BEING WITH CHILDREN (New York: Doubleday, 1975); Parsons, T., "Age and sex in the social structure of the United States," in Eisenstadt, S.N.(ed.), FROM GENERATION TO GENERATION (Glencoe, Ill.: Free Press, 1956); Reich, C., THE GREENING OF AMERICA: THE COMING OF A NEW GENERATION (Glencoe, Ill.: Free Press, 1966), THE MAKING OF A COUNTER CULTURE (Garden City, N. Y.: Anchor, 1969).

2. French, J. R., and Raven, B. H., "The basis of social power," in Cartwright, D. (ed.) STUDIES IN SOCIAL POWER (Ann Arbor, Mich.: University of Michigan, 1959).

3. Bayh, B., CHALLENGE FOR THE THIRD CENTURY: EDUCATION IN A SAFE ENVIRONMENT, Final Report on the Nature and Prevention of School Violence and Vandalism (Washington, D. C.: U. S. Government Printing Office, 1977).

4. Deutsch, M., MINORITY GROUP AND CLASS STATUS AS RELATED TO SOCIAL AND PERSONALITY FACTORS IN SCHOLASTIC ACHIEVEMENT, Society for Applied Anthropology Monograph, 1960.

5. The literature is extensive but a few should be listed: Bettelheim, B., "Individual and mass behavior in extreme situations," JOURNAL OF ABNORMAL AND SOCIAL PSYCHOLOGY, 38: 417-452, 1943; Goffman, E., ASYLUMS: ESSAYS ON THE SOCIAL SITUATION OF MENTAL PATIENTS AND OTHER INMATES (Garden City, N. Y.: Anchor, 1961); Gouldner, A., PATTERNS OF INDUSTRIAL BUREAUCRACY (New York: Free Press , 1954) and WILDCAT STRIKE (New

York: Harper, 1954); Rawick, G. P., THE AMERICAN SLAVE: A COMPOSITE AUTOBIOGRAPHY (Westport, Conn.: Greenwood, 1972); Schein, E. H., "Brainwashing," in Bennis, W. G., Schein, E. H., and Steel, F. I., (eds.) INTERPERSONAL DYNAMICS (Homewood, Ill.: Dorsey, 1946).

6. Hillery, G. A., "Freedom and social organization: A comparative analysis," AMERICAN SOCIOLOGICAL REVIEW, 36: 51-65, 1971; and Hillery, G. A., and Klobus, P. A., "Freedom in confined populations," Unpublished manuscript, Virginia Polytechnic Institute and State University.

7. Hillery, G. A., and Lincoln, A. J., "Leisure, freedom, and crowd behavior," JOURNAL OF LEISURE RESEARCH, in press.

8. SCHOOL STOPPERS TEXTBOOK: HANDBOOK FOR SCHOOL DISRUPTION AND VIOLENCE, (Washington, D. C.: U. S. Government Printing Office, reprint).

9. Bowles, S., "Unequal education and the reproduction of the social division of labor," in Carnoy, M. (ed.) SCHOOLING IN A CORPORATE SOCIETY (New York: David McKay, 1972); Cobb, J. and Sennett, R., THE HIDDEN INJURIES OF CLASS (New York: Alfred A. Knopf, 1972); Jencks, C. INEQUALITY: A REASSESSMENT OF THE EFFECT OF FAMILY AND SCHOOLING IN AMERICA (New York: Basic Books, 1972). Schrag, P. and Divoky, D. THE MYTH OF THE HYPERACTIVE CHILD AND OTHER MEANS OF CHILD CONTROL (New York: Pantheon, 1975).

DELINQUENT BEHAVIOR IN THE PUBLIC SCHOOLS: TOWARD MORE ACCURATE LABELING AND EFFECTIVE INTERVENTION

Ronald A. Feldman, Ph.D.
Director
Center for the Study of Youth Development
Boys Town, Nebraska

and

Professor of Social Work
George Warren Brown School of Social Work
Washington University
St. Louis, Missouri

Whether regarded as a primary or a secondary factor, it is evident that inaccurate social labeling plays a determinant role in the etiology of deviant behavior among public school students. The difficulties associated with most systems for labeling youth have led some observers to advocate their total elimination(1). It is suggested here, however, that many if not most of the deficiencies of contemporary labeling systems can be remedied. Consequently, it is possible to construct more effective approaches toward intervention in the public schools, thus vitiating some of the important causal factors that lead to delinquent behavior among students.

LABELING IN THE PUBLIC SCHOOLS

In a landmark study of social labeling Nicholas Hobbs set forth a number of basic assumptions regarding the need for effective systems of classifying youths, including public school students. Hobbs assumes, first, that some means of classifying malfunctioning youths is essential in order to plan and organize helping programs, obtain services, and assess outcomes of intervention efforts. Unlike some investigators, he does not believe that classification efforts should be abandoned.

> "*Although we understand that some people advocate the elimination of classification in order to get rid of its harmful effects, their proposed solution oversimplifies the problem . . . We shall address abuses in classification and labeling, but we do not wish to encourage the belief that abuses can be remedied by not classifying. In fact, we shall argue for more precise categories and for more discriminating ways of describing children in order to plan appropriate programs for them, and we shall advocate safeguards to decrease the deleterious effects of classification procedures that can, in fact, have many beneficial outcomes*" (2).

Hobbs' second assumption is that public and private policies and practices must manifest respect for the individuality of children and appreciation for their diverse talents and cultural backgrounds. Third, he posits that there is growing public concern over the use and abuse of categories and labels, particularly as applied to children, and that there is widespread dissatisfaction with inadequate, uncoordinated, and hurtful services for children and youth. And fourth, he believes that special programs for labeled youth, including delinquents, must be designed to encourage their full participation in normal growing experiences (including regular schooling and recreational activities and normal family and community life). When a youth must be removed from normal activities, he should be removed the least possible distance in time, in geographical space, and in the psychological texture of the experience provided.

Hobbs notes also that frequently there is a discrepancy between a youth's measured capacity and his functional competence. Moreover, the growth patterns of youngsters are rapid and irregular, so that any label may be invalidated, with or without special treatment, by the passing of time and growth of the child. Additionally, special treatment programs for children often are neither effective nor benign. Students placed in special classes seldom return to regular classrooms, and youngsters placed in institutions are likely to bear their mark forever. Consequently, regardless of which classification system is employed, when labeled youngsters are admitted to special programs that separate them from normal peers, explicit provisions must be made for periodic review of their status in order to restore them to regular settings as quickly as possible.

Given the above assumptions, and the evident need for effective classification and labeling systems, the challenge before social scientists and school administrators is a complex one: namely, how to retain the benefits of labeling while diminishing its negative consequences. Specifically, how can public school personnel develop labeling systems for children and youth which, on the one hand, will weaken those forces which generate and sustain dysfunctional deviant behavior and, on the other, will optimize needed intervention efforts to help students who already have embarked upon deviant careers? Such systems are critically needed in order to limit the interaction between adverse public school labeling processes and the emergence or retention of delinquent behavior patterns (3).

The following discussion focuses particularly upon the problems and the potentials of social labeling in the public schools. Problems of contemporary labeling systems are reviewed first. A descriptive typology of labeling systems used in the public schools then will be presented. This discussion is followed by a number of recommendations designed to promote more effective social labeling and intervention in public school systems.

PROBLEMS ASSOCIATED WITH CONTEMPORARY LABELING SYSTEMS

The deficiencies of contemporary labeling systems are manifold. Traditional labeling categories usually yield too little information to plan a course of action for a student. Descriptions such as "predelinquent," "oppositional," "aggressive," or "status offender" tell school personnel far too little about a youth's actual behavior problems. Correspondingly, they offer little guidance for intervention efforts. When a student displays multiple behavior problems, as delinquents often do, classification in accordance with some dominant set of attributes may lead to neglect of other conditions much in need of attention.

Social labels may err in either of two directions. First, those who impute a deviant label to a student may exaggerate, or *over*label the extent of his deviant behavior. Alternatively, there may occur significant under-attribution, or *under*labeling of deviant behavior — a phenomenon which has been neglected somewhat by investigators but which, nonetheless, must be viewed as an integral feature of society's failure to analyze and deal adequately with the dysfunctions of contemporary public school systems. Global labels reveal little about the precise *types* of deviant behavior(s) exhibited by a student, the *seriousness* of those behaviors, the *frequencies* of their occurrence, or their *social context.*

Unfortunately, today it can hardly be said that there exists a true theory of social labeling. Instead, the available knowledge regarding this phenomenon approaches, at best, the requirements for a theoretical frame of reference. That is, currently there exist only a limited number of variables and empirical referents pertaining to social labeling. Moreover, the conceptual interrelationships among such desiderata tend to be poorly delineated. There are but few hypothesized interrelationships among the primary variables and these seldom have been tested through systematic empirical investigation. It is likely, therefore, to be quite some time before there evolves a comprehensive conceptual scheme which demonstrates the breadth, depth, and sophistication worthy of the denotation of "theory."

Nonetheless, there are emergent signs of a coherent knowledge base about social labeling. Ultimately, it should be possible to apply this knowledge in order to gain better understanding about the interrelationships between public schools and juvenile delinquency. It will be necessary, however, for second-order concepts of social labeling to be elaborated and operationalized.

These should account for the multifaceted and multidimensional nature of social labeling. In addition, such multivariate features should apply to all basic components of the labeling process, namely, the *labelee(s)*, the *labeler(s)*, their respective situational or *social context(s)*, and the *reciprocal interactions* among all of the foregoing. Wherever possible both the qualitative and quantitative features of the labeling process and its basic components must be identified and operationalized.

TOWARD A LABELING TYPOLOGY

Progress toward development of a true theory of social labeling can be expedited through the elaboration of relevant conceptual typologies. Although these may exhibit such rudimentary features as dichotomous categories or other nominal-order characteristics, it is likely that they will evolve into more precise interval-order and ratio-scale schemata. For illustrative purposes one such format will be described here. Its basic features are drawn from a discussion set forth elsewhere (4) which focuses primarily upon the derivation of social role typologies for disabled persons. For heuristic purposes, the format has been extended in order to demonstrate one approach to elaboration of social labeling typologies that can be applied in public school contexts for purposes of diagnosis and intervention.

Among the basic elements of social labeling are the behavioral attributes of both the labeled individual and those who label him. Most social labeling studies focus upon one or the other of these variables. Although substantial literature exists about self-attributional phenomena such as self-image (5) and self-concept (6), there appear to be relatively few investigations of the interrelationships among such variables, individual behavior, and the attributions of relevant others. Especially lacking are studies of the extent to which self-attributions and others' attributions are congruent or synchronous, and of the ways in which such synchronies are related to various types of accurate or inaccurate behavioral definitions.

The basic components of the labeling typology set forth here are (1) the actual behaviors of the labeled individual (that is, the student), (2) the labels which the labeled student applies to himself, and (3) the labels which relevant others (that is, school teachers) apply to the student. As suggested in Table I, it is assumed to be empirically possible, using clinical, normative, or other standards, to ascertain whether a given individual's behavior can be regarded as normal or deviant. Although behavior should be viewed in terms of multidimensional continua, the dichotomous definition of behavior as "normal" or "deviant" will serve here as a basis for derivation of a nominal-order typological framework.

TABLE I

**VARIETIES OF ACCURATE AND INACCURATE SOCIAL LABELING
BY SELF (STUDENT) AND OTHERS (TEACHERS)**

	Label Attributed By Others (Teachers)	
Student Behavior is Normal	Normal	Deviant
Label Attributed by Self (Student)		
Normal	I. True normalcy	II. Imposed deviance
Deviant	III. Autistic deviance	IV. Fictionalized deviance
Student Behavior is Deviant		
Label Attributed by Self (Student)		
Normal	V. Fictionalized normalcy	VI. Autistic normalcy
Deviant	VII. Imposed normalcy	VIII. True deviance

Although a student's behavior in fact may be within normal ranges, it is possible for him to regard his own behavior as either normal or deviant, depending upon the acuity and appropriateness of his self-attributions. Clearly, a well-adjusted student will ascribe normalcy to himself if his behavior is, in fact, normal. In other instances, however, functionally normal individuals may ascribe to themselves abnormal or deviant behaviors and attributes (e.g., hypochondriasis). Similarly, when a student's actual behavior can be defined objectively as deviant it is possible for him to ascribe to himself either normal or deviant behaviors and attributes. A student who describes himself as deviant when, in fact, he behaves in a deviant manner may be far better adjusted than one who views himself as normal under such circumstances.

Regardless of an individual's perceptions of his own behavior, attributions by his peers and by others who engage in social interaction with him tend to occur. The latter, too, may view the labeled individual as behaving in either a normal or a deviant manner. Moreover, the attributions of relevant others may or may not be congruent with objective definitions of the labelee's actual behavior. It is desirable, for example, that a student who behaves in a normal manner be so defined by relevant others, particularly his teachers. Likewise, it is desirable and appropriate for a student who behaves in a deviant manner to be defined as such by others in his environs, including teachers.

On occasion, however, the converse may occur. Some students who behave normally may be incorrectly viewed as deviant by their peers, teachers, or parents. Such may be the plight of the "good" boy in a group of "bad" peers. Similarly, it is conceivable for an individual who comports himself in a deviant manner to be considered normal by others. Relevant examples include the eccentric genius and the constructive revolutionary. However, regardless of the fit between actual behavior and the attributions of others, it is possible for the labeled individual concurrently to hold self-attributions which may or may not be congruent with his actual behavior or the attributions of relevant others.

It is important, then, to recognize that teachers and others can define a labeled student's behavior in a manner which is dissonant or nonveridical with respect to his *actual* behavior. This insight serves as the basic point of departure for labeling theorists. Simply stated, relevant individuals in a student's environment in effect can certify that he acts in an "abnormal" manner despite countervailing objective indicators. Similarly, a child may be certified as "normal" despite objective evidence to the contrary. In accordance with the basic premises of labeling theory such reference group definitions may induce, for better or worse, subsequent behavior by the labeled individual consonant with those definitions. This etiological phenomenon is considered to underlie much delinquent behavior (7). From a more adaptive standpoint, it has been viewed as the major contributing factor to many therapeutic cures, faith healings, and "placebo effects" (8).

The juxtaposition of these three major variables (the labeled student's self-attributions, the attributions of his teachers, and his actual behavior) may result in the elaboration of an eight-fold typology. This typology permits assessment of the extent to which accurate or inaccurate labeling occurs in public schools (see Table I). In those instances where both the labeled student and his teachers define the student's behavior identically, it can be said that *attribution synchrony,* or *labeling synchrony,* has occurred. Such may be the case when both sets of labelers (that is, student and teachers) define the student's behavior as normal or, likewise, when both define it as deviant. When synchronous attributions are congruent with objective definitions of the labelee's actual behavior *valid* attribution synchrony obtains. This is depicted in Cells I and VIII of Table I. When synchronous attributions are not congruent with objective definitions of the labeled student's actual behavior *invalid* attribution synchrony exists, as in Cells IV and V of Table I. Hence attribution synchronies may be either valid or invalid.

Invalid attribution synchronies probably represent an unbalanced or dissonant socio-behavioral state somewhat analogous to the cognitive dissonance posited by social psychologists (9). Unlike instances of valid attribution synchrony, invalid attribution synchronies may shift gradually toward less dissonant or more balanced socio-behavioral states. Given the congruent attributions of self and others, it seems probable that the labeled student's actual behavior will shift in the general direction of the conformity-inducing attributions. Shifts in the attributions of either the labeled individual or relevant others appear unlikely since they would exacerbate, rather than reduce, the extent of socio-behavioral dissonance.

There also may be certain instances when a labeled student and his teachers hold attributions concerning the student's behavior which are at variance with one another. For example, teachers may view a student as deviant while the student views himself as normal, or vice versa. Such instances, which exemplify *attribution asynchrony,* are likely to constitute the most stressful and least stable of all socio-behavioral situations. Strong pressures to reduce the accompanying discomfiture probably will be alleviated by a shift in the child's self-attributions toward those held by the majority of relevant others (10). This is especially likely if large numbers of teachers and/or peers unanimously challenge the self-attributions of the labeled student (11). If relevant others are few in number, or if they substantially disagree among themselves, there is a greater likelihood that the labeled child will retain his own self-attributions and, indeed, that one or more of the others will resolve the dissonance by shifting their attributions toward congruence with those of the labelee.

It is possible to classify the respective types of asynchronies and valid and invalid attribution synchronies denoted in Table I. For example, a situation of "true normalcy" will obtain when the student's actual behavior is normal and when teachers and the student both regard such behavior as normal (Cell I). The obverse, that is, when the student's behavior is deviant and both he and his teachers label his behavior as deviant, may be regarded as "true deviance" (Cell VIII). "True normalcy" and "true deviance" both represent instances of valid attribution synchrony. They will be among the most stable of all possible situations and least subject to subsequent change in terms of either behavior or corresponding attributions. The six remaining socio-behavioral situations, or cells illustrated in Table I, represent less stable situations that will be correspondingly more susceptible to subsequent alterations.

Cell II represents a situation in which the student's behavior is objectively defined as normal and he views it as such. In this case, however, teachers discrepantly attribute deviant behavior to the student, resulting in "imposed deviance." This represents the classic form of dysfunctional labeling described in the delinquency literature. As readily demonstrated by the typology, it represents only one of many possible types of social labeling. This observation points clearly to the rather undeveloped conceptual state of the current literature about labeling in school systems.

Cell VII illustrates another variation of imposed behavioral definitions, namely, "imposed normalcy." This situation occurs when a student's actual behavior is deviant, when he correctly labels such behavior as deviant, but when teachers label him as normal. An example might be the case of a pupil with self-recognized behavioral or learning difficulties, but who goes unnoticed by the teacher in a class with far too many students. The potentially dysfunctional consequences for the labeled student are obvious. The situation represents an attribution asynchrony which may be detrimental to the student who, unfortunately, assesses himself more accurately than do important others in his immediate social environment.

Somewhat different examples of attribution asynchrony are represented by Cells III and VI. In the former case, the labeled student may behave normally and may be labeled as normal by teachers; however, he has labeled himself as deviant, resulting in an instance of "autistic deviance." An analogous situation occurs when the labeled student manifests deviant behavior, is viewed appropriately as deviant by teachers, but considers himself to be normal (Cell VI). This represents a situation of "autistic normalcy." Since these illustrations represent attribution asynchronies they are unlikely to remain stable. Because of his minority position, it is likely that the labeled student ultimately will change his self-attributions or his behavior – most probably the former – in order to resolve the socio-behavioral dissonance. This supposition, and all others presented here, represents a testable hypothesis that can indicate the fruitfulness of the typology and its potential contributions toward a theory of social labeling.

Finally, instances may occur when a student behaves normally but both he and his teachers view such behavior as deviant. This situation, represented in Cell IV, may be defined as "fictional deviance." Conversely, the labeled student may exhibit deviant behavior, but be subjected to attributions of normalcy by both himself and his teachers. Such a situation, illustrated in Cell V, may be termed "fictionalized normalcy." Each of these situations represents an invalid attribution synchrony. Although the respective attributions of the labeled student and his teachers are congruent, or synchronous, they clearly are discrepant with the labelee's objectively evaluated behavior and, therefore, are invalid. Because of the synchronous nature of the attributions, such situations are more stable and less subject to remediation than the attribution asynchronies represented by Cells II, III, VI, and VII. Nonetheless, they entail some stress which ultimately may be alleviated, most likely through subsequent behavioral changes which, on occasion, may be quite detrimental to the student.

The foregoing typology represents but one illustration of a means for extending conceptual frameworks about social labeling and applying them in public school systems. Such conceptions can further the development of a broad-based theory of social labeling, help to generate testable hypotheses, and facilitate evaluation and documentation of essential components of labeling theory. It is anticipated that over time they will become more multivariate and multidimensional in nature. Moreover, they are likely to evolve towards more quantifiable conceptual frameworks, based primarily upon interval or ratio scales. At this point, however, it may be useful to indicate how current knowledge about labeling can lead to more effective intervention.

TOWARD BETTER LABELING AND INTERVENTION IN THE PUBLIC SCHOOLS

Effective intervention in the public schools will require substantial progress toward identification and quantification of key socio-behavioral labeling referents. Labeling systems must be characterized by a number of features. First, interventions based upon social labeling must be drawn from a valid knowledge base which is generated primarily by empirical investigation. Second, such knowledge must be characterized by predictive potency. A given proposition about social labeling should be embedded within propositions linked by logical relations that permit genuine derivations.

The key variables of labeling systems should be characterized also by variable potency. Variables may be potent or weak, depending on how much empirical variance they account for in social labeling. Similarly, as Cromwell *et al.* note, they must satisfy the criterion of "coverage" (12). This refers to the degree to which the classificatory terms cover, or are directly applicable to, the population of individuals classified. Key variables also must meet the criterion of reliability and, as such, must be reproducible in a variety of contexts. The corresponding measurement schemata must be discrete, precise, objective, and, above all, amenable to multiple and repeated tests by a variety of judges or observers.

As Thomas has noted, the intervention utility of a given knowledge base depends largely upon features of the referents associated with it (13). If knowledge about social labeling is to be useful, the necessary referents should be characterized by identifiability and accessibility. These are prerequisites if referent manipulability is to be achieved. An important related factor is the manipulation cost of a referent. Even when a referent is manipulable in principle, the requisite interventions may be prohibitively costly.

In addition to the above desiderata, a number of steps should be taken in order to assure precise labeling and social intervention. Teachers should undergo training to enable them to understand the complexities, implications, and potential uses of social labeling. If this is not possible, they should delegate their labeling responsibilities to those who are so trained. Labels must be highly specific yet, in total, they must represent an exhaustive inventory of each student's problem behavior. *All* relevant instances of deviant behavior should be recorded. They should be arrayed by type of deviant behavior, seriousness of the behavior, the social context of the behavior, and the frequency of its occurrence per unit of time.

The latter should be defined through the use of valid and reliable measurement procedures. These should be based upon appropriate time-sampling methods and should entail reliability checks by a variety of independent judges (such as parents, guidance counselors, or peers). These independent judges should use similar formats for recording their observations and report their judgments to the teacher. In addition to providing verifications of deviant behavior, such procedures may be of immense diagnostic value insofar as they reveal situational or temporal variations in a student's pattern of deviance. To the extent that these objectives are achieved they will help to diminish broad-scale stereotyping and stigmatization of students. Finally, at predetermined intervals teachers should be obliged to review a student's behavior, status, and concomitant label(s). Accordingly, they should expunge an adverse label from a student's record so long as proper gains have been made. This safeguard will neutralize the invidious tendency to prolong incorrect labels beyond the period for which they are truly valid.

Once accurate definitions of a student's deviant behavior are formulated, an effort should be made to prescribe interventions that can reduce or eliminate such behaviors. Otherwise the labeling process, even if accurate, is likely to be of little avail. Intervention need not concentrate upon the target student alone. For maximum effectiveness intervention might focus also upon parents, peers, or others who are integrally linked with the student's maladaptive behavior. The criteria and methods used for evaluating the student's deviant behavior also should be used for evaluating the effectiveness of the prescribed intervention. Once an accurate label is affixed it should be removed only when it is no longer valid; ideally, this should occur after the requisite interventions have resulted in student improvement. Preferably, the removal of a meaningful label should be accomplished by the same individual(s) who originally affixed it, namely, the teacher or guidance counselor. Finally, for maximum effectiveness, those school personnel who affix and remove significant student labels should be systematically and objectively evaluated for the quality of their own performance. Only through such safeguards can a school system assure the expertness of its labeling agents and properly guarantee their acceptance by students, parents, and professional colleagues.

SUMMARY

Knowledge about social labeling has proliferated immensely within the past decade. From relatively naive, limited, and unidimensional formulations there have evolved sophisticated, comprehensive, and multidimensional ones. These trends have been complemented by increasing recognition of the critical relationship between knowledge about labeling and the elaboration of effective public school programs, whether they be of an habilitative or rehabilitative nature.

The present discussion has sought to identify key problems associated with contemporary public school labeling systems. A descriptive typology for public school labeling was formulated and recommendations were set forth in order to promote more effective social labeling and intervention in school systems concerned about the delinquent behavior of students.

FOOTNOTES

1. Schur, E. M. RADICAL NON-INTERVENTION: RETHINK-ING THE DELINQUENCY PROBLEM. Englewood Cliffs, N.J.: Prentice-Hall 1973.
2. Hobbs, N. (ed.) ISSUES IN THE CLASSIFICATION OF CHILDREN. San Francisco: Jossey-Bass, 1975.
3. Vinter, R. D. and Sarri, R. C. "Malperformance in the Public School: A Group Work Approach," SOCIAL WORK, 1965, *10*, 3-13; Schafer, W. E. "Deviance in the Public School: An Interactional View," in E. J. Thomas (ed.), BEHAVIORAL SCIENCE FOR SOCIAL WORKERS, New York, Free Press, 1967.
4. Thomas, E. J. "Problems of Disability From the Perspective of Role Theory," in E. J. Thomas (ed.), BEHAVIOR-AL SCIENCE FOR SOCIAL WORKERS, Glencoe: Free Press, 1967.
5. Katz, P., and Zigler, E. "Self-Image Disparity: A Developmental Approach." JOURNAL OF PERSONALITY AND SOCIAL PSYCHOLOGY, 1967, *5*, 186-195; Rosenberg, M. SOCIETY AND THE ADOLESCENT SELF-IMAGE. Princeton: Princeton University Press, 1965; Sarri, R. C. "Self-Image Perspectives of Delinquents in Custodial and Treatment Institutions," in E. J. Thomas (ed.), BEHAVIORAL SCIENCE FOR SOCIAL WORKERS. Glencoe: Free Press, 1967.
6. Reckless, W., *et al.*, "Self-Concept as an Insulator Against Delinquency." AMERICAN SOCIOLOGICAL RE-VIEW, 1956, *21*, 744-746; Coombs, R. H. "Social Participation, Self-Concept, and Interpersonal Valuation." SOCIOMETRY, 1969, *32*(3), 273-286; Fannin, L. F., and Clinard, M. B. "Differences in the Conception of Self as a Male Among Lower and Middle Class Delinquents." SOCIAL PROBLEMS, 1965, *13*(2), 205-213; Rosenberg, M. "Parental Interest and Children's Self-Conceptions." SOCIOMETRY, 1963, *26*(1), 35-49; Schwartz, M., *et al.*, "A Note on Self-Conception and the Emotionally Disturbed Role."

SOCIOMETRY, 1966, *29*(3), 300-305; Tangri, S. S., and Schwartz, M. "Delinquency Research and the Self-Concept Variable." JOURNAL OF CRIMINAL LAW, CRIMINOLOGY, AND POLICE SCIENCE, 1967, *58*(2), 182-190.

7. See, for example, Akers, R. L. "Problems in the Sociology of Deviance: Social Definitions and Behavior." SOCIAL FORCES, 1968, *46*(4), 455-465; Eisner, V. THE DELINQUENCY LABEL: THE EPIDEMIOLOGY OF JUVENILE DELINQUENCY. New York: Random House, 1969; Erikson, K. T. "Notes on the Sociology of Deviance." SOCIAL PROBLEMS, 1962, *10*, 307-314; Schur, E. M. LABELING DEVIANT BEHAVIOR. New York: Harper and Row, 1971; Short, J. F., Jr. "Differential Association and Delinquency." SOCIAL PROBLEMS, 1957, *4*, 233-239; Werthman, C. "The Function of Social Definitions in the Development of Delinquent Careers," in President's Commission on Law Enforcement and Administration of Justice, TASK FORCE REPORT: JUVENILE DELINQUENCY AND YOUTH CRIME. Washington, D. C.: U. S. Government Printing Office, 1967.

8. Fish, J. M. PLACEBO THERAPY. San Francisco: Jossey-Bass 1973; Frank, J. D. PERSUASION AND HEALING: A COMPARATIVE STUDY OF PSYCHO-THERAPY. Baltimore: Johns Hopkins Press, 1961; Rosenthal, R. EXPERIMENTER EFFECTS IN BEHAVIORAL RESEARCH. New York: Appleton-Century-Crofts, 1966.

9. Festinger, R. L. THEORY OF COGNITIVE DISSONANCE. Evanston, Illinois: Row, Peterson, and Company, 1957.

10. Backman, C. W., Secord, P. F. and Peirce, J. R. "Resistance to Change in the Self-Concept as a Function of Consensus Among Significant Others," in C. W. Backman and P. F. Secord (eds.) PROBLEMS IN SOCIAL PSYCHOLOGY. New York: McGraw-Hill, 1966.

11. Asch, S. SOCIAL PSYCHOLOGY. Englewood Cliffs, N.J.:

Prentice-Hall, 1952; Feldman, R. A. "An Experimental Study of Conformity Behavior as a Small Group Phenomenon." SMALL GROUP BEHAVIOR, 1974, 5(4), 404-426.

12. Cromwell, R. L., Blashfield, R. K., and Strauss, J. S. "Criteria for Classification Systems," in N. Hobbs (ed.), ISSUES IN THE CLASSIFICATION OF CHILDREN, VOLUME I. San Francisco: Jossey-Bass, 1975.

13. Thomas, E. J. "Selecting Knowledge From Behavioral Science," in BUILDING SOCIAL WORK KNOWL-EDGE: REPORT OF A CONFERENCE. New York: National Association of Social Workers, 1964. Also in E. J. Thomas (ed.), BEHAVIORAL SCIENCE FOR SOCIAL WORKERS, Glencoe: Free Press, 1967, 417-424.

SCHOOL-COMMUNITY LINKAGES:
AVENUES OF ALIENATION OR SOCIALIZATION

Jacqueline Scherer
Oakland University
Rochester, Michigan

Delinquency has been defined as a "troublesome orientation" suggesting a "willingness to engage in forms of behavior, especially peer behavior, which render the individual vulnerable to punishment and sanction by adults (1)." Youths who have such an orientation can be said to be alienated — a state representing a serious breakdown in socialization or a "mutual divorce between the individual and society (2)."

If delinquency can be viewed as a socialization problem, then its causes and cures may be explicated by examining society's agencies of socialization and the delinquent's relationships to them. In such an examination, the school will be a primary focus, for, as John Dewey pointed out in 1897, the goals of education and of socialization are closely related:

> "*Education being a social process, the school is simply that form of community life in which all those agencies are concentrated that will be most effective in bringing the child to share in the inherited resources of the race, and to use his own powers for social ends (3).*"

Dewey also noted that for socialization to occur, or for people to come to hold the values of a common culture, there must be adequate communication (4). Effective socialization requires that socializing agencies share a common purpose and a common responsibility and that communication among them be open and continuous.

Unfortunately, most contemporary socialization organizations, both formal and informal, do not perceive Dewey's commonality of purpose nor do they accept a shared responsibility for social tasks. Their relationships, in fact, are characterized more by hostility, competitiveness, and isolation than by common purpose — a divisiveness and lack of communication which provide avenues of alienation for young people. Juveniles who come in contact with several different socialization organizations thus encounter inconsistency, uncoordinated activities, and communication breakdowns. And those who "slip between the cracks" of organizations are only too likely to find pathways to delinquency and crime.

Study of social networks — or the linkages between and among individuals, groups, agencies, and organizations (5) — can help in the prevention of delinquency by identifying points at which linkages are weak or nonexistent and the ways in which communication among units of socialization can be improved. An examination of the social network of the typical public school may help educators, and others concerned with the school's role in delinquency prevention, to identify and correct inadequacies in communication and cooperation between the school and other agencies and institutions affecting youth.

THE SOCIAL NETWORK OF THE SCHOOL

From descriptions of school-community relations in the literature and reports of current research it is possible to construct a model of a school social network which is typical of most communities. Analyses of social networks may include measures of the density of the network, or the number of contacts and frequency of contacts between two points; the range of contacts, with measures of the degree of overlap or scope; the durability of contacts over time; and the intensity or psychological potency of the contacts. From such measures one can make judgments about the strength or weakness of different parts of the network; estimate the efficiency of various channels and linkages between points; and begin to make tentative statements about the qualitative dimensions of contacts.

The "domain" of the school includes all formal instructional services for youth between ages six and 16, or grades K – 12. In this context, the term domain means the organization's locus in a field, including not only its goals, resources, and activities but also important ideological dimensions (6). Since compulsory school attendance laws legitimize the school's domain and create formal ties between the school and virtually all youth, the school is highly visible within any community. Strong legitimization and a high profile combine to make the school the most powerful formal institution of socialization in the community, second in influence only to the family.

Schools generally are dominant in their contacts with other agents of socialization; school staff initiate most contacts and limit them, as much as possible, to formal situations located in the school building. Parent involvement, for example, is structured within the Parent-Teacher Association or occasional school visits, usually clearly identified by such devices as requiring parents to obtain "visitor" passes. The volume of organizational contacts between youth groups and schools is surprisingly low (7) considering the enormous number of contacts between individual youths and the school. Since other socialization organizations deal with only a fraction of the total youth population on a more informal basis, they are less able to regulate the format or volume of contacts and are vulnerable to client withdrawal.

The types of contacts initiated by schools reflect their powerful position. On the one hand, the school can claim that its domain is restricted to "academic" matters, while on the other it can claim to serve "the whole child." In this way the school can add or substract from its domain with more ease than other socialization organizations, particularly those dealing with disruptive youth. The definition of responsibility may become very narrow for disruptive youth whereas it can be expanded to broadly accommodate the development of more acceptable young people.

Even a cursory description of the social network of the

school reveals the strength of the school's position in terms of frequency of formal contact, isolation of the school from other socialization organizations and agencies, and the relatively close connection between school and family. A sharp contrast between the quality of family ties and those between the school and other community organizations can be seen. Family ties are affective, characterized by the personal, supportive, responsible, and sustained contact which is essential for human development and behavioral change. The linkages between the school and other organizations or individuals are just the opposite: bureaucratic, rather than personal; formal instead of mixed; more regulative than supportive, rigid instead of responsive, more intermittent than sustained; and characterized by specialized and independent rather than cooperative and mutually reinforcing activities.

Several important questions emerge from these observations: How can school personnel establish productive linkages with families? Are there other natural informal linkages between school and community socialization organizations? How can the frequency of student contacts with the school be used to redesign the social network? Is there a difference between the voluntary ties of an individual with other community organizations and his involuntary ties with the school? Although more research is needed to adequately address these questions, some strategies for improving school-community linkages can be suggested.

IMPROVING SCHOOL-COMMUNITY LINKAGES

This view of the school within a socialization network suggests some approaches to improving the socialization process by concentrating on linkages in the network. These include: (1) increasing the number of linkages between the school and other agencies of socialization; (2) using a variety of channels for contact; (3) formally recognizing shared responsibilities in socialization; (4) extending the range of the socialization network; (5) developing more liaison staff; (6) reducing the impact of negative linkages; (7) conducting research and other analyses of social networks.

INCREASING THE NUMBER OF TIES

An obvious strategy for improving the school's social network is to increase the number of linkages between the school and the community. School critics have argued for such a change, demanding that school walls be torn down. Some advocate the "deschooling" of society and the destruction of "hard" walls (8); others simply want to reduce the isolation of the schools and "soften" the walls (9), but almost all decry the artificial barriers between school and community. Specific ways to increase ties are:

1. *Utilize school space for community socialization organizations.* For example, locate youth assistance offices or city recreation department offices in school buildings, or provide space for personnel from voluntary socialization organizations, such as churches, to assist youth. This is done regularly for social workers and, in many large cities, police counselors; but the idea can be expanded to include a variety of socializing agents and organizations.

2. *House crisis centers within school walls.* Modest success has been reported with peer counseling centers operating within regular school programs, and the idea of school "crisis" has as much validity as any other. Intervention centers which provide coordinated services to youth can be developed (10).

3. *Develop formal and regular linkages between the school and other community organizations.* It might be useful to view this as a process, starting with informal cooperation and moving into regularized and formal agreements. Weinstein and Morover (11) have developed a typology of the four patterns of organizational relationships found in health and welfare organizations which could be applied to the socialization network. These categories are:

a. Informal cooperation — e.g., client referrals,

information exchanges, professional consultations, and service planning.

b. Formal cooperation — e.g., written agreements providing for personnel exchanges, material exchanges, patient transfers, and counseling services.

c. Formal purchase agreements — one organization agrees to purchase services from another, recognized in a contract of specified duration, usually listing the hours of service and a certain percentage of an employee's time. The goal here is to avoid duplication of services or staffs when the volume of demand for such services is low.

d. Coordinated services — two or more organizations working together in joint programs, shared facilities, or pooled resources to provide a package of services.

Weinstein and Morover note that "public central, public local and private endowed organizations have high boundary control because of their stable channels of funding (12)." Schools also have been able to remain isolated for this reason, entering into organizational relationships only when forced to do so by community pressures or state law.

4. *Encourage informal inter-organizational ties at the middle level of the organization.* Teachers and agency staff can meet in community groups. The emphasis upon management participation in such groups as the Junior Chamber of Commerce, Kiwanis, Rotary, United Fund, and Welfare planning groups is well established in both industry and commercial organizations, but school representation has generally been restricted to high-level administrators. Teachers could be relieved of class-room responsibilities on occasion to attend such meetings and school representatives can be encouraged to participate in social policy boards by accepting this as a regular part of the job. Community involvement could become as much a part of the professional development of school teachers as it has become for academic staff of universities. In a similar fashion, agency representatives can become regular participants in school activities, assisting in curricula policy development and other school concerns.

USING VARIED CHANNELS FOR CONTACT

An examination of existing channels between the school and other community groups reveals that the most numerous, as well as the shortest, channels between the school and families are those followed by students. Underutilization of these effective linkages is wasteful. Use of students to tie the school to agencies and organizations in the community also is a practical and effective way to involve students in the socialization process. Student involvement, which can operate on both formal and informal levels, also will facilitate the first strategy: increasing the number of linkages or ties.

Prominent educational critics have noted the importance of involving students more actively in school and community organizations, citing the importance of developing autonomy, learning the skills of group work, and becoming involved in meaningful activities. The National Commission on Resources for Youth has encouraged participatory programs for young people in both school and community programs. Youth participation is defined as "involving youth in responsible, challenging action that meets genuine needs, with opportunity for planning, and/or decision making affecting others, in an activity whose impact or consequences extends to others — i.e., outside or beyond the youth participants themselves (13)." Other ideas are the Integrated Community Education System (14) which enables students to become "partners in research" within the local community; the Open Partnership (15) which leads to shared decision-making by everyone concerned with education; and a growing number of work-study vocational education programs which include student internships outside the class. The goal of most of these efforts is to actively engage students in the socialization process. The Panel on Youth (16) concluded that the best way of encouraging young people to take on more responsibilities, "to interact with people across a broader range of ages and circumstances, and to expand their work-role experiences," was to decrease the time that young people spend in formal educational settings (17). It was also suggested that the federal government provide funds for "host" organizations in the community.

RECOGNIZING SHARED RESPONSIBILITIES

Most staff do not view themselves as providing social services, a perspective which is made possible by the nature of school financing. In recent literature on inter-organizational relationships in the social services, schools are discussed only marginally. Most citizens do not see the problem of welfare financing as related directly to the issues of educational funding, and the debates over accountability to date have not directly linked academic services with other specialized social services. As a result, the schools' interpretation of their domain has been relatively unchallenged. It is unlikely that schools will voluntarily redefine existing domain assumptions, although it may be possible to encourage voluntary cooperation between schools and community organizations.

The lack of official recognition of the shared domain in youthful socialization has made it impossible to design good follow-up programs. Young people who have experienced difficulties in particular socialization organizations (such as offenders, disabled learners, disruptive youth, or medically handicapped juveniles) generally have not received the necessary follow-up services (18). While schools have effectively withstood most pressures to assume more responsibility for students in non-academic areas, many students are simply pushed out by administrative rules for expulsion or suspension.

Support and feedback, two essential requirements for resocialization efforts requiring strong network linkages, can be provided through organized self-help groups; professional crisis counseling; reference group support to encourage change; and other valuable but informal unorganized support systems (19). The goal is to increase the "social capital" of these youngsters so that they have many sources of support. All members of the socialization network should be held accountable for follow-up and follow-through with problem-oriented young people.

113

EXTENDING NETWORK RANGE

Increasing the number of ties and the overlap between organizations will make socialization networks more dense, but the range of these networks also can be extended. Schools have remained aloof from important socialization activities occurring outside their immediate domain. The most blatant example of this has been television, which clearly plays a potent role in the intellectual, emotional, and character development of young people. Until recently, school administrators and teachers have been silent regarding the quality or quantity of television viewing. Parent-teacher groups have become increasingly concerned, but school officials remain reluctant to participate in coordinating programs or supervise the development of media policies.

Another area in which the school remains uninvolved is that of recreation. Except for the participation of young people in formal school sports programs or officially sanctioned school activities, school staff generally do not support recreational programs. One source of this reluctance may be the fact that many schools are required to provide transportation for students who engage in school-supported recreational events; yet Boards of Education seldom request funds for improved public transportation so that recreational programs can be further developed. Strategies which require school staff to cooperate actively with other socialization organizations within the community and beyond its borders may make school personnel more aware of the importance of their work to the task of education. Such strategies include school staff on governing boards of community groups; community seminars on youth; planning commissions regulating and designing policies to coordinate activities; and official recognition of mutual responsibilities in socialization.

EXPANDING LIAISON STAFF

Another strategy for increasing school-community linkages is to develop more liaison staff and to design more creative roles for such personnel. The growing interest in youth advocacy represents one such effort. Youth advocates can effectively espouse the interests of individual youth, crossing the boundary lines of many socialization organizations and refusing to accept a limiting definition of their role. Outreach workers (community aides, attendance staff, social workers, or whatever else they may be called) can provide a continuous flow of information across channels.

One danger in any liaison role is that the actor will not be given sufficient autonomy to operate effectively. When this occurs, he or she becomes an instrument of administrative policies without an independent base. To a large extent this has happened to school guidance counselors who spend most of their time testing, screening, and guiding students into school tracks rather than operating between home and school or linking various areas of the student's life. There is some value in officially recognizing such a role within a school, but to be effective liaison staff must be given sufficiently high status to effect real change. Also, practical support must follow liaison efforts in the form of resource commitment; thus, implementing liaison strategies requires high-level involvement and attention.

REDUCING NEGATIVE LINKAGES

It would be misleading to assume that all school-community linkages have positive results. For example, there is often unofficial collusion between police and school staffs which diminishes student trust in all official organizations. Business contacts also may restrict school perceptions in such important areas as curricular development. Many peer contact groups either do not discourage delinquency or actually support it. It is important to analyze network contacts for their negative and positive qualities and to develop strategies which reduce the number of negative contacts or increase their distance from the school.

RESEARCHING SCHOOL NETWORKS

Empirical investigations must be undertaken to test the

115

validity of any model. Most school and community organization staffs are unaware of the real nature of their contacts within the socialization network and tend to overestimate some contacts while underestimating others. It is important that serious efforts to identify and document contacts be undertaken on a systematic basis. Some analyses are exceptionally difficult but, in the long run, are worth the effort. Studies of peer networks, for example, can be useful in developing support systems and in finding programs which reduce negative contacts. The relationship between the family and the school also should be studied to provide a basis for using natural support systems to reinforce resocialization efforts. The methodology of network research ranges from complex mathematical modeling and highly sophisticated computer techniques to simple but systematic observation of what occurs in schools and community organizations. In all research the key to success is not quantity or sophistication, but careful attention to empirical reality.

The literature on juvenile delinquency also suggests strategies that begin with organizations serving offenders or with social services agencies dealing with youth. For example, Knudten (20) suggests that delinquency prevention specialists be included on state and local school boards; that teachers be trained in delinquency prevention; that school administrators attend in-service institutes on delinquency prevention; and that there be incentives for the schools to keep delinquents enrolled in school. Whether one begins with the school or with other community organizations, the goal is to increase the number, depth, and range of contacts between and among all agencies of socialization.

CONCLUSION

Because of its powerful position in the community, the school is a natural center of any socialization network. Unfortunately, this power can be used to stifle change by keeping innovation within the bounds of institutionalized structures, by co-opting personnel of other organizations, or by dominating community decision-making processes. Inadequate linkages between the school and other socialization organizations produce a reluctance to acknowledge problems of youth in school, a pattern of blaming others for problems, and a tendency to develop artificial boundaries to isolate schools as well as complex coping strategies to deal with perceived threats to their domain.

The effects of uncoordinated socialization can be seen in the ways in which young people use the compartmentalized socialization structures to conceal information, to avoid responsibility, and to express frustration and alienation when their needs are continually unmet. It is not unreasonable to conclude that the divisions between and among the agencies and organizations intended for their socialization reveal the inauthenticity of society's commitment to youth.

FOOTNOTES

1. Polk, K., "Schools and the delinquency experience," in DELINQUENCY PREVENTION AND THE SCHOOLS: EMERGING PERSPECTIVES, CONTEMPORARY SOCIAL ISSUES, Vol. 29, Ernst Wenk, Editor, Sage Publications, 1976.
2. Rhodes, W., and Tracy, M. (eds.), A STUDY OF CHILD VARIANCE (Ann Arbor: University of Michigan, 1974), 2 vols.
3. Dewey, J., "My pedagogic creed," reprinted in Gezi, K. and Meyer, J. (eds.),TEACHING IN AMERICAN CULTURE (New York: Holt, Rinehart, and Winston, 1968).
4. Dewey, J., THE PUBLIC AND ITS PROBLEMS (New York: Holt, Rinehart, 1929).
5. See Laumann, E., PRESTIGE AND ASSOCIATION IN

THE URBAN COMMUNITY (Indianapolis: Bobbs, Merrill, 1966); and Litwak, E., and Meyer, H., "The school and the family: Linking organizations and extended primary groups," in Lazarfeld, P., Sewell, W., and Wilensky, H. (eds.), THE USES OF SOCIOLOGY (New York: Basic Books, 1967).

6. Warren, R., Rose, S., and Bergunder, A., THE STRUCTURE OF URBAN REFORM: COMMUNITY DECISION ORGANIZATIONS IN STABILITY AND CHANGE (Lexington: D. C. Heath, 1974).

7. *Ibid.*

8. Illich, I., DESCHOOLING SOCIETY (New York: Harper, 1971).

9. Oliver, D., EDUCATION AND COMMUNITY: A RADICAL CRITIQUE OF INNOVATION SCHOOLING (Berkeley: McCutchen, 1976). Also Friedenberg, E., "The modern high school: A profile," in L. Drabick (ed.), EDUCATION: A SOCIOLOGICAL APPROACH (New York: Appleton-Century-Crofts, 1971).

10. Powell, W. C., "Educational intervention as a preventive measure," in DELINQUENCY PREVENTION AND THE SCHOOLS: EMERGING PERSPECTIVES, CONTEMPORARY SOCIAL ISSUES, Vol. 29, Ernst Wenk, Editor, Sage Publications, 1976.

11. Weinstein, R., and Morover, J., "A comparative analysis of health and welfare organizations," PACIFIC SOCIOLOGICAL REVIEW 20(1):79-103, 1977.

12. *Ibid.*, p. 98.

13. National Commission on Resources for Youth, N.Y. NEWSLETTER 4(11):1975.

14. Wenk, E., "Introduction" and "Schools and the community: A model for participatory problem solving," in DELINQUENCY PREVENTION AND THE SCHOOLS: EMERGING PERSPECTIVES, CONTEMPORARY SOCIAL ISSUES, Vol. 29, Ernst Wenk, Editor, Sage Publications, 1976.

15. Ryan, C., THE OPEN PARTNERSHIP: EQUALITY IN RUNNING THE SCHOOLS (New York: McGraw-Hill, 1976).

16. Coleman, J. S., *et al.*, YOUTH: TRANSITION TO ADULT-HOOD. Report of the Panel on Youth of the President's Advisory Committee (Chicago: University of Chicago, 1974).

17. Adams, J., UNDERSTANDING ADOLESCENCE: CURRENT DEVELOPMENTS IN ADOLESCENT PSYCHOLOGY (Boston: Allyn and Bacon, 1976).

18. Rothman and Walker, "Continuity of care between the psychiatric hospital and public schools," in Franklin, P. and R. (eds.),TOMORROW'S TRACK:EXPERIMENTS WITH LEARNING TO CHANGE (Boston: New Community, 1976). The authors discovered that 75% of all psychiatric professionals never follow up a client once he or she returns to school.

19. Warren, D., BLACK NEIGHBORHOODS: AN ASSESSMENT OF COMMUNITY POWER (Ann Arbor: University of Michigan, 1975).

20. Knudten, R., "Delinquency programs in schools: A survey," in DELINQUENCY PREVENTION AND THE SCHOOLS: EMERGING PERSPECTIVES, CONTEMPORARY SOCIAL ISSUES, Vol. 29, Ernst Wenk, Editor, Sage Publications 1976.

VALUE ORIENTATIONS AND DELINQUENCY:
A THEORETICAL SYNTHESIS

Stephen A. Cernkovich
R. Serge Denisoff
Department of Sociology
Bowling Green State University

Within the voluminous literature on juvenile delinquency two relatively distinct theoretical models have tended to dominate: structural theory and control theory. Although the importance of the school in the etiology of delinquency is emphasized by both, these models offer quite different accounts of the genesis and maintenance of delinquent behavior patterns and thus have different implications for delinquency prevention.

Structural theories stress the importance of social-class position and access to legitimate opportunities in the causal processes which lead to delinquency (1). Social-class position is viewed as important primarily because it sets in motion particular "delinquency-producing" processes. The argument is relatively straightforward if somewhat oversimplified here: Lower-class adolescents find that socially approved avenues to success are not available to them, or else that they are severely restricted; they turn to delinquency as a reaction to frustrated goal-seeking or as an alternative means of achieving desired goals. In general, then, structural models suggest that when access to legitimate means of reaching culturally defined success goals is blocked or when the individual is not equipped to compete effectively for social rewards, processes are set in motion which create pressures toward delinquency involvement.

Control theory, in contrast, suggests that many adolescents are insulated from involvement in delinquent activities by conventional value commitments (e.g., belief in the worth of formal education, hard work, delayed gratification, and so forth); and that it is the weakening of such conventional commitments, coupled with the development of a hedonistic, fun-seeking adolescent lifestyle, which makes delinquency a likely occurrence. Although many factors typically are involved, value orientations are central to most control theories. In general, two sets of value orientations are considered: conventional value orientations (e.g., overt, formal, official values such as deferred gratification, practicality, the worth of formal education, etc.) (2); and "subterranean" value orientations (e.g., covert, informal, unofficial values such as short-run hedonism, excitement, trouble-seeking, toughness, etc.) (3). The argument is that conventional value attachments tend to inhibit delinquency involvement because they reflect a stake in conformity (4), while subterranean value attachments tend to induce delinquency involvement, if only as a by-product of excitement-seeking behavior (5). In other words, as a result of withdrawal of commitment to conventional values, and in the course of hedonistic activities, delinquency becomes much more likely.

The role of the school is relatively clear, although often implicit, in both structural and control theories. In structural models it is the school setting, and the unequal competition for status within it, which generates the deprivations and frustrations leading to delinquency involvement. Lower-class students, who are especially ill-prepared to achieve success in school, develop an alternative status system — a system which confers status for delinquent or disruptive behaviors — in which they can compete on an equal footing (6). In this sense, delinquency provides a functional alternative to the conventional status system, or at least a means of striking back at what is viewed as an unjust system. According to control theory, commitment to school and to the conventional lessons it teaches tends to "insulate" youth from involvement in delinquency. For example, students who accept the demands of deferred gratification required for success in school may avoid delinquent behavior because they do not want to jeopardize their future opportunities with a police record. It is when such commitment to conventionality is weakened or broken (for whatever reason) that the individual is likely to engage in delinquent activities (7).

If for no other reason, the sheer amount of time a youth spends in school and in school-related activities cannot help but importantly shape his values, attitudes, and behavior — delinquent or otherwise. That the school is viewed as differentially related to juvenile delinquency depending on the theory to which one happens to subscribe indicates the complexity of its relationship to delinquency involvement, but it also suggests that integrating the two major theoretical explanations of delinquency may add significantly to our understanding of juvenile misconduct and the role of the school in its causation (8).

DELINQUENCY INVOLVEMENT: A SYNTHESIS

The theoretical model presented here represents an attempt to build a synthesis of structural and control theories by concentrating on the relationship between value orientations and delinquency involvement. In the process, an effort is made to reconcile the apparent conflicts between the two models and to resolve a longstanding discrepancy between explanations of lower-class delinquency (usually structural theories) and those which purport to explain delinquency among middle-class youth (primarily control theories).

The fact that lower-class delinquency appears to be more frequent and more serious has led many sociologists to infer uncritically that the causes of this behavior must be different somehow from the causes of middle-class delinquency, which is viewed as being less serious and frequent. Yet if delinquency is viewed as ". . . a continuum of behavior, ranging from some very serious acts of law violation to other conditions which are relatively innocuous or benign" (9) it is possible to see that delinquent behavior by adolescents of all social classes may be an expression of the same value orientations. A comparison of lower- and middle-class delinquency, in fact, does lend support to this contention. The values specified by some researchers as critical to the development of delinquent behavior patterns among lower class (10) are identical to those found by others to lead to middle-class delinquency (11). Thus it can be seen that values and their expression in behavior may constitute essential elements in the explanation of delinquency, regardless of social class position.

A schematic representation of the proposed theoretical synthesis is presented in Figure 1. It is suggested that while the variables of social-class position and perception of available opportunities indeed are important factors, the relationship of these two factors to delinquency has been oversimplified in structural theories. Rather than directly causing delinquency (which is the impression left by structural models), it is likely that the effect of these two variables is indirect and in a specific causal sequence. First, a youth's position in the class structure is likely to affect his perception of the opportunities available to him for reaching specific goals. Generally, the lower the social-class standing of the individual, the greater the likelihood that he will perceive blocked or limited access to legitimate educational and occupational opportunities. This is consistent with research which suggests that lower-class youth simply do not have effective, socially approved access to the opportunities available to higher-status adolescents or that lower-class youth often have not been sufficiently prepared by their socialization experiences to compete successfully according to the middle-class rules of the game.

The role of social-class position, however, can be overplayed. The perception of limited opportunities is dependent on far more than class position; and it is quite likely that middle-class, and even higher status adolescents, may perceive restrictions on their effective opportunities (12). For example, regardless of class position, many adolescents view their experiences in school as irrelevant to the achievement of future goals. Thus, perception of limited access to genuine opportunities is much more significant in delinquency causation than is social-class position *per se.*

It is postulated that the way in which perception of limited opportunities leads to delinquency is through its effect

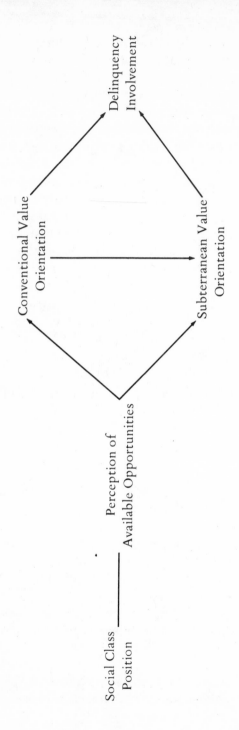

FIGURE 1: A SYNTHESIS OF DELINQUENCY CAUSATION THEORIES

on commitment to conventional values and involvement in conventional activities. This is the case almost by definition since legitimate opportunities are defined in terms of conventional activities and values: If a youth finds that conventional standards and norms are functional for the achievement of his goals, he will be likely to maintain his commitment to them; if not, commitment is likely to be withdrawn. For example, if a youth views his school-related activities as having neither short-run benefits (such as eliciting praise and other rewards from teachers or from peers) nor long-range pay-offs (if school is seen as unrelated to future occupational, vocational, or educational goals), it can be expected that commitment will be quite weak, if for no other reason than the fact that conventional values and norms are viewed as relatively useless in seeking important individual goals.

Just as the perception of ineffective or blocked opportunities may contribute to the withdrawal of commitment to conventional values, it also is likely to generate a commitment to substitute, subterranean values as more effective in achieving both short- and long-range goals. Both of these developments tend to increase the likelihood of delinquency — the former by reducing or eliminating the inhibiting effect of commitment to conventional values (13), the latter by exposing the individual to unconventional activities which are likely to be either delinquent or conducive to delinquency.

To summarize the model up to this point, then, social-class position affects the individual's perception of the opportunities available to him for reaching certain goals, and this view of the opportunity structure in turn affects degree of commitment to conventional values. It is the latter which has the most immediate effect on delinquency, with strong adherence to conventional values tending to inhibit delinquency involvement and weak commitment tending to make delinquency a much more probable outcome. Further, to the extent that an individual finds that conventional values do not "work" for him, he will be in the market for other values which are functional. As Rainwater has noted, few adolescents will maintain strong adherence to conventional values "despite their inability to achieve satisfactorily in terms of them (14)." Rather, for those who find that they are blocked from successful goal achievement via conventional values and norms, the stage is set for the development of substitute values and norms which offer reasonable opportunities for success.

The very nature of the substitute, subterranean values almost insures involvement in some form of delinquency. For example, if an individual is committed to "toughness" as an important means of proving his masculinity, or for achieving status among his peers, the odds are high that he will become involved in aggressive behavior or fighting, the seriousness of which will depend on the relative saliency of the value. Similarly, a strong commitment to "thrill-seeking" insures involvement in various hedonistic activities, some of which are likely to go beyond the bounds of acceptable behavior. But it is the combination of a weakening or withdrawal of commitment to conventional values and the development of a strong adherence to subterranean values which is likely to lead to delinquency involvement. To the extent that values serve to guide and direct action, it is expected that they will find frequent expression in behavior, delinquent or otherwise. When conventional values are first rejected and then replaced by unconventional or subterranean values, the likelihood of involvement in delinquent or predelinquent activities is markedly increased (15).

PRACTICAL IMPLICATION OF THE MODEL

The model presented above suggests that value orientations are the most significant determinants of behavior in general and of juvenile delinquency in particular. Value orientations can be viewed as standards of desirability or criteria for selection among alternative courses of action as well as justifications for behavior. They operate to direct, channel, and rationalize behavior and all but the most meaningless behaviors reflect at least a minimal orientation to values (16). Any treatment or control strategy, therefore, should be directed at value orientations with the intent of creating, sustaining, and/or strengthening among individuals a "stake in conformity" — that particular value configuration which inhibits frequent or serious involvement in delinquent activities.

The school is in a particularly good position to affect an adolescent's stake in conformity. The amount of time a student spends in the classroom and the significance of his successes and failures in school and in school-related activities suggest that these particular social arrangements can importantly influence value orientations and thus either induce or inhibit delinquency involvement. A number of ways in which school personnel may be able to influence students in the direction of a nondelinquent lifestyle can be suggested.

On the most general level, teachers and other school personnel should avoid characterizing students as either "good" or "bad" on the basis of isolated instances of misbehavior. A youth found guilty of a single act of theft or vandalism, for example, should not necessarily be labeled a "trouble-maker" or a "hard-core delinquent." There is much evidence to indicate that the vast majority of adolescents at some time commit a delinquent act but, in most cases, such misconduct is both infrequent and relatively minor. It would, of course, be similarly mistaken to view the "good student" as one who is never involved in delinquency — he probably is. The good-boy/bad-boy characterization not only is an inaccurate reflection of reality but it serves to perpetuate a self-fulfilling expectation in which those defined as "bad" end up being bad because they see no point in trying to conform. Rather than changing their behavior, those labeled as "bad" are likely to become increasingly bitter, frustrated, and resentful. Such an outcome is obviously antithetical to the development of a commitment to conformity.

School personnel also are in a position to affect students' perceptions of available opportunities. We have argued that an individual's evaluation of available opportunities significantly affects his value commitments, which, in turn, are important determinants of the likelihood of his involvement in delinquent activities. For many youth who are involved in frequent and serious delinquency, not only does the school provide many frustrating experiences, but those opportunities which are available often are viewed as irrelevant to the achievement of important goals. Another common complaint of students is that they are permitted little or no input into the development of school programs. The implication is that a greater degree of meaningful student participation in the planning and development of both academic and extracurricular programs would make school a more relevant and certainly more rewarding experience. Further, since student input would reflect their own criteria of relevancy, students are likely to be committed to programs they help to create because such programs are likely to be viewed as allowing them to secure present and future goals. In any effort to involve students in program development it is crucial to include students of varied backgrounds (although this is not always a simple task) rather than only a select few, and to offer several different options since one or two programs cannot be expected to meet the needs of a diverse school population. Our model suggests that such involvement would not only restore and maintain a "stake in conformity," but also would negate the necessity to turn to subterranean values as an alternative means of reaching success-goals, or as a reaction to the perceived irrelevancy of existing arrangements.

Finally, it is important to take seriously the ideas, aspirations, and expectations of adolescents, whether or not we understand or agree with them. Adults too often have failed to set examples of conformity which adolescents can emulate or to instill any lasting commitment to conventional values. Many social theorists have remarked on the hypocritical nature of American society — the tendency of adults to preach the gospel of conformity while engaging in less than conforming behavior themselves. It is surely unreasonable to expect adolescents to conform when adults set such frequent examples of nonconforming behavior. Contradictory expectations and the prevailing double standard serve only to exacerbate the problem of youthful misbehavior. Parents, teachers, and other adults can significantly impact the values — and thus the behaviors — of adolescents on a daily basis by maintaining some degree of consistency between what is said and what is done and by explaining the existence of different standards or inconsistencies between values and behavior whenever these appear. This approach would seem to offer a sound means for reducing the general tendency toward involvement in delinquency by attacking the problem at its source: the value orientations of youth.

FOOTNOTES

1. See, for example: Cloward, R.A. and Ohlin, L.E., DELINQUENCY AND OPPORTUNITY: A THEORY OF DELINQUENT GANGS (New York:Free Press, 1960); Cohen, A.K., DELINQUENT BOYS (New York: Free Press, 1955); Merton, R.K., "Social structure and anomie," AMERICAN SOCIOLOGICAL REVIEW, 3:672-682, 1938.
2. Cohen, *supra* note 1; Williams, R.M., Jr., AMERICAN SOCIETY: A SOCIOLOGICAL INTERPRETATION, 2nd ed. (New York: Knopf, 1960); and Williams, R.M., Jr., "Individual and group values," In Gross, B.M. (ed.), SOCIAL INTELLIGENCE FOR AMERICA'S FUTURE (Boston: Allyn and Bacon, 1969).
3. England, R.W., Jr., "A theory of middle-class juvenile delinquency," JOURNAL OF CRIMINAL LAW, CRIMINOLOGY AND POLICE SCIENCE, 50:535-540, 1960; Matza, D. and Sykes, G.M.,"Juvenile delinquency and subterranean values," AMERICAN SOCIOLOGICAL REVIEW, 26:712-719, 1961; Miller, W.B., "Lower class culture as a generating milieu of gang delinquency," JOURNAL OF SOCIAL ISSUES, 14:5-19, 1958; Scott, J.W. and Vaz, E.W., "A perspective on middle-class delinquency," CANADIAN JOURNAL OF ECONOMICS AND POLITICAL SCIENCE, 29:324-335, 1963.

4. Cohen, *supra* note 1. See also: Cohen, A.K., "Middle class delinquency and the social structure," in Vaz, E.A. (ed.), MIDDLE-CLASS JUVENILE DELINQUENCY (New York: Harper and Row, 1967); and Hirschi, T. CAUSES OF DELINQUENCY (Berkeley: University of California Press, 1969).

5. Miller, *supra* note 3; and Matza and Sykes, *supra* note 3.

6. Cohen, *supra* note 1.

7. Hirschi, *supra* note 4.

8. The theoretical model developed in this paper is based on data derived from anonymous self-report questionnaires administered to a representative sample of 412 male high-school students in a medium-sized midwestern city. A more detailed statistical treatment of the data, including information on questionnaire items and scale construction, is available in Cernkovich, S.A., "Value orientations and delinquency involvement," CRIMINOLOGY: AN INTERDISCIPLINARY JOURNAL, 15:443-458, 1978; and Cernkovich, S.A., "Evaluating two models of delinquency causation: structural theory and control theory," forthcoming in CRIMINOLOGY: AN INTERDISCIPLINARY JOURNAL.

   We are also indebted to the earlier work on delinquency and the schools by Walter E. Schafer and Kenneth Polk ("Delinquency and the Schools," pp. 222-277, TASK FORCE REPORT: JUVENILE DELINQUENCY AND YOUTH CRIME, Washington, D.C.: U.S. Government Printing Office, 1967) for providing a comprehensive framework within which we could develop our theoretical model as well as make specific recommendations for treatment and control.

9. Gibbons, D.C., DELINQUENT BEHAVIOR (Englewood Cliffs: Prentice Hall, 1970), p.11.

10. Cohen, *supra* note 1; Miller, *supra* note 3.

11. Cohen, *supra* note 4; Kvaraceus, W. and Miller, W.B., DELINQUENT BEHAVIOR: CULTURE AND THE INDIVIDUAL (Washington, D.C.: National Educa-

tion Association, 1959); and Scott and Vaz, *supra* note 3.

12. Cernkovich, *supra* note 8.

13. This is clearly consistent with control theory. See: Cohen, *supra* note 4.

14. Rainwater, L., "The problem of lower class culture," JOURNAL OF SOCIAL ISSUES 26:133-148, 1970.

15. This conclusion is constructed on the work of Cohen, *supra* note 1, England, *supra* note 3, Rainwater, *ibid.*, Scott and Vaz, *supra* note 3, and Matza and Sykes, *supra* note 3.

16. Kluckhohn, C., "Values and value-orientation in the theory of action," In Parsons, T. and Shils, E.A. (eds.), TOWARD A GENERAL THEORY OF ACTION (New York: Harper and Row, 1951); Kohn, M.L., CLASS AND CONFORMITY: A STUDY IN VALUES (Homewood, Ill. Dorsey Press, 1969); Rokeach, M., BELIEFS, ATTITUDES AND VALUES (San Francisco: Jossey-Bass, 1969); Williams, R.M., Jr., "The concept of values," In Sills, D.L. (ed.), INTERNATIONAL ENCYCLOPEDIA OF THE SOCIAL SCIENCES (New York: Macmillan and the Free Press, 1968); and Williams, *supra* note 2.

HUMAN RELATIONS TRAINING IN SCHOOL SETTINGS

Chester W. Oden, Jr.
W. Scott MacDonald
University of Minnesota

INTRODUCTION

While Human Relations training generally is based on four principles, and hence, such training has similarities from one school to another, it is not possible to articulate the specific program for any school because the needs of each school must be ascertained individually and the program tailored to those needs. This point can be simplified by reviewing the four principles underlying Human Relations training:

1. Each individual, with his/her particular learning history, is a unique person and must be considered in this uniqueness.
2. All persons in the United States tend to be raised in a national philosophy of racism.
3. Schools are social structures with many common elements; most have reflected in their structure the recognition of status differentials based on physical appearances (racism).
4. Each school has a structure reflecting the particular sets of talents of its administration.

These underlying assumptions can be challenged. It is certainly possible that all persons in a school, for example, might not be prejudiced. In our experience, however, we have found varying degrees of prejudice in all schools. Assuming these principles to be true, the need for a training program tailored to the individual needs of each school is clear. While prejudice and institutional racism are common to all schools, there are differences

between schools in terms of school structure and in the interpersonal actions of each individual. The term "prejudice" is a
descriptor indicating a social structure with status differential
based on appearance. This is not an invidious term nor is it
meant as a moral judgment. We assume, in fact, that every
person in the United States is prejudiced to varying degrees. In
prejudice, we all begin at the same point.

CHARACTERISTICS OF THE HUMAN RELATIONS
TRAINING PROGRAM

There are two types of concerns around which training
programs are built: a) The institutional concerns include assessment of the operation of the school to ascertain decision-making processes, criterion for distribution of rewards and resources, and, b) the personal concerns which encourage teachers
to be ever on the alert about their own biases.

An assessment is made of the school before the Human
Relations Training program is begun.* This begins with the
notification by the institution that Human Relations Training is
requested and involves an evaluation of the school as a structured social unit with regulations, informal communication
system, ongoing social processes, an official communication
system in which directives and decisions are disseminated. This
appraisal requires the interaction of training staff and representatives of administration, office staff, teachers, and students.
Generally, the assessment precedes any final plan for training. A
large part can be done via questionnaires filled out prior to the
scheduled sessions.

Part two of the assessment is ongoing. Training involves
each member of the school looking into him/herself for sources
of prejudice. Administrators undergo self-examination by
reviewing policies, practices and projects they have which

*This article is based on Human Relation Training Programs
developed at the Human Relations Program, University of
Minnesota, Minneapolis, MN.

might advantage one group or another. Office personnel can assist in this self-examination by reviewing their operations in terms of processing requests, detention slips, etc. and in their own dealing with individuals. Teachers can ask themselves about subject content, as well as individual and group interactions with students and fellow faculty.

During these activities, it is not anticipated that either individuals, or the school as a social structure will undergo any changes which are discernible from the outside. Indeed, the purpose of this period is to introduce individuals to the process of soul-searching so that when training begins, this internalization process will have already begun.

Human Relations Training is very personal. Some of those who undergo this experience will find it strenuous and even painful, in a psychological sense. The assessment aspect should begin as early as possible. Efforts extended during this phase will pay large dividends for those who enter into the training later.

Training involves the entire school personnel. There are some sessions which involve the administrators, teachers, and the office personnel as homogeneous groups (in terms of school activities), and some sessions in which groups will be heterogeneous. One type of meeting continues from the assessment phase and deals with social problems identified by the school staff. In a second type of meeting, individuals are asked to deal with specific school issues and react in the situation honestly in a continuing effort to discover biasing practices. Facilitators especially qualified for Human Relations Training assist in this process.

PREPARATION FOR TRAINING

Preparations for the training begin when first contact is made with the facilitators. It is essential to decide at the outset that proper time, space, and personnel are available in order to meet objectives. Normally the schools making the request have some specific objectives: the trainers also have objectives which must become inculcated into the program for it to have maximum input. Schools are generally enthusiastic about the added objectives. When both parties are satisfied that the program requested is consistent with the training available, a contract arrangement is established. First discussions should concern the school's stated objectives. It is during this discourse that the individual nature of training becomes apparent. Each school has its own individual problems, perceived needs, and objectives. Often further examination uncovers individual needs of the school depending on the make-up of the faculty, the students, and the array of situational factors impinging on the school from the population base of the community to the perceived expectations of the school by the business community.

Questionnaires are prepared for teachers and administrators. Some aspects dealing with job-related activities demand different sorts of questions. Questionnaires are prepared from the preliminary discussions with school officials. Questions include requests for general problems the school has, to those individual problems encountered by teachers. The idea of the questionnaire is to solicit specific reactions about the day-to-day operations of the school personnel and to elicit each staff member's view of the school's current status and needs.

The second thrust is to ascertain the administrative flow of the school. What are hiring and advancement policies in the school? Who gets what assignments? What sorts of activities on the part of students and teachers are encouraged — both on paper and in reality? How are academic materials selected? Who handles discipline? What are the discipline problems of the school? What liaison is there between community and the school? What sort of support does the school receive from community, as well as from its parent structure?

The training staff then combs the questionnaires and interview data and begins to assemble a picture of the school and its daily operations. The discussion of the training plan for the school develops along two lines: the structural line, and the individual line. The structural line follows after the picture of the school's operation is developed. Each school has a distinct style of administration. This is first articulated and discussed with school officials. The training team ascertains the decision making processes; who makes what decisions. Such questions as, "does everyone know who makes this or that decision" are asked, and implications examined. Then, the communication flow is examined. Is the school traditional (with a generally downward flow) or is it a "horizontal" structure (where administrators share with teachers or committees the authority and responsibilities for assessing problems, posing questions and reaching decisions)? What are the implications for this particular system? What are the problems faced by the administration, and are there biases in the current solutions generally achieved by administration? This part of the planning examines the paper flow, the talk flow, and the nonverbal flow of influences which generate administrative impact concerning the dispersal of school's resources. These processes are clarified with the school administration, so that the relationship between assessment and realities of the situation, as well as plans for suggested solutions can be maintained. This process is normally very useful and often results in updating of school procedures.

MISBEHAVIOR AND SCHOOL ADMINISTRATION

When examining administrative procedures, school misbehavior becomes especially important. Generally, we have found that school administrators are extremely conscientious about administrative practices vis-a-vis those students who break rules. It is often this very conscientiousness that needs closer examination.

The Human Relations perspective demands a review of ongoing cases and/or detailed review of past problems. While it would appear from the discussion that there are two distinct realms of training, that of the personal, and that of the social structure, in reality they are really so closely intertwined that one cannot be easily distinguished from the other. The most effective way we have found to deal with the interface of personalities with school policy is through the discussion of specific cases. Normally, school administrators are willing to bring out and dust off difficult cases. Occasionally we deal with cases having certain characteristics in common: those in which minority students or faculty have been involved, even in seemingly tangential cases. When we make it clear that minority includes ethnic differences, women, persons with various beliefs, and those with physical or mental handicaps, there is little trouble in recalling instances.

A review of cases involving minority persons is central to the Human Relations training. We find that, almost inevitably, the school policies and administration become intertwined with individual thoughts, feelings, values and assumptions. And, we may find biases in this examination. Some personnel are "protecting" minority students and as a result do not give them room for growth experiences. Other personnel exhibit discriminatory practice against minorities. Either of these can be expected to lead to problems. We may find that school personnel, trained in the traditional American culture (in which the white, male values and standards prevail as "best" and any deviation from that is considered "bad" and, hence, to be remediated) are opposing the growth of students, staff, or community members with non-white male values. It is only as long as the school staff is unaware of its biases that the problems normally prevail. This is because the school staff assumes that rules and processes should be implemented equally for all. But as the needs of minorities are unraveled, and as the thoughts of administrators or teachers are examined more closely, decisions which foster growth can be elicited and the problems often evaporate. Examination of special cases may involve accusations and recriminations, but interpersonal conflicts are resolved and shared relationships are actually strengthened as a result. In our experience, we find that fault assignment is useless and sidetracks the solution of problems. It is the discovery of hidden assumptions, partially hidden expectations and values on the part of school personnel as well as students and parents that maintains problems. Bringing into focus these partially obscured mental and emotional processes permits the reasonable and prompt resolution of problems.

Unwinding the almost incomprehensible tangle of issues in school crime involves a tearing apart of issues involving those misbehaviors which are stimulated by the school processes, and those which are a result of school-independent matters. But distinctions between school-fostered and non-school fostered crime are difficult to ascertain unless a keen knowledge exists regarding the nature of the student population and the school faculty. Some schools have crime which is stimulated nearly solely by on-campus activities. Others deal with crime which is stimulated by the life on the streets surrounding the school. Schools face the task of becoming the corrections agency for the community. Yet other schools find themselves in a complex tangle of crime stimulated by a clash of elements in the surrounding community which is brought into the school each morning. Each of these situations must be dealt with in context of the nature of the problem.

This is why pretraining assessment is essential. And this is why some instruction may be conducted in parts of three days, and others involve a year-long "project" type of human relations training program to begin to untangle the issues in which the school, itself, may not be the principal actor.

DEVELOPMENT ISSUES IN HUMAN RELATIONS TRAINING

While the basic issues in a given school district may remain constant, the form may vary slightly from elementary through high school grades. Biases hold out across age in unexpected ways. Whether we have prejudices regarding minority groups is not necessarily related to the prejudices we hold regarding pupils of various ages. Whether or not we choose to let young students develop independence is a problem unto itself, as are other problems of maturation. The independence and assertiveness individuals must develop may be intertwined with ethnic or sexual differences. Sexual development in students as they enter their teens, the proximity to adulthood and subsequent concern for vocational independence may be a problem for some teachers.

We are not saying that teachers are expected to be outstanding examples of perfect adjustment in every part of their lives. Children, at different ages, move from one type of developmental need to another, and require correspondingly, different talents from their teachers. The teacher who is excellent with kindergarteners, in their first absences from home, may be poor with teenagers who need increasing independence in decision-making.

POPULATION CHANGES

In the last two decades, our society has seen staggering changes in the characteristics of populations in various geographical areas. As the characteristics of neighborhoods change, so do the characteristics of children in schools. In the face of such population changes, the administrations and faculties of schools tend to retain a more stable characteristic. Schools retain middle-class orientations, with values on book-learning and economic mobility. Further, specific schools often take on particular characteristics: the faculty may prize college entrance, or vocational specialty. When such a school exists in the flux-and-flow of a neighborhood undergoing a change in population characteristics, the community and school may well find themselves caught in a tug of war regarding the mission of the school. It is easy for the faculty of a school to begin to take pride in emphasizing athletic achievement, or scholastic excellence. While such pride may be an indication of accepting community values one year, it may be the root of problems with the community several years hence when the needs of the community alter. It is possible for pride to become entrenched and to serve as anchors for personal values, hence the roots of prejudice.

It is valuable for Training teams to gain a clear awareness of these social change problems. The problems between school and community may be minor ones of expectations regarding homework, to major ones concerning the value to be placed on

English as the primary language and what is acceptable behavior versus what isn't acceptable.

THE ROLE OF THE SCHOOL

Related to the above is the role of the school. While it is sometimes very difficult to determine, it is often vitally important to find what the parents of students feel is the role of the school. Again, this may vary widely. At one extreme, some schools serve students from white middle class families. In such schools it is as if parents are teaching their own children. No problems stem from values clashes. But a significant number of schools operate along traditional white middle class orientations but deal with students from non-white and/or non-middle class families. In such cases, the agreement regarding what is expected of the students may be a major stumbling block. Who is responsible for the conduct of the students? What is the major task of the school regarding the students? What do the parents do when their children are acting at odds with what is expected from school faculty? The questions mount, and frustrations can become deeply ingrained problems unless mutual expectations are clarified.

Up to now, we have discussed some of the steps which precede the Human Relations Training in schools. When the information has been collected, and the goals have been laid out to the satisfaction of school administration, teachers, and training personnel, two types of training then ensue.

INDIVIDUAL TRAINING

One type of training focuses on individual performance. This is done in groups, though it should not be confused with sensitivity, encounter or other types of group training. Instruction is focused on the performance of teachers, counselors, and administrators in the discharge of their duties in a Human Relations framework.

Underlying all training is a basic strategy. It has been our experience that most of the school personnel have sincere and persistent desires to free themselves of prejudices. Indeed, many insist that they have NO prejudices. We first try to gain tentative acceptance of the idea that each of us, having been raised in a nation whose history and traditions have been ones of prejudice, should not be expected to be without prejudice. Indeed, we assert that each person has prejudice and should not be ashamed of it. It is only when we either ignore our prejudices and have our performance influenced by it, or when we actively engage in discriminatory behavior (resulting from prejudice) that we bring problems to the school. Further, that those who wish to maintain prejudices against one group or another should simply volunteer not to work with the group toward which the prejudice exists. The point of our work is to assist in awareness of prejudice, and to set about neutralizing the effects of prejudice in teaching practices.

The training plan may involve combinations of approaches for helping participants achieve more effective functioning. After introductory procedures which induce comfort and dedication to meet the objectives of the meetings, the group may be asked to look at problem films in which groups of students are in conflict situations. Group members may be asked to describe similar instances in their school, to propose the roots of the problem, as well as short and long term solutions. During such discussions the values and preconceptions of the participants become evident, and are a part of the strategies for solutions. Another time, content materials may be examined with strengths and weaknesses of the academic program reviewed. Again, preferences and aversions of faculty become evident, and when faculty bring these biases into focus, they may quickly move to make curriculum changes to offset deficiencies or discriminations. Participants may play "round robin" in which each indicates a way in which that participant will improve his/her work in the future. Role playing can also be used. The techniques of the trainer are selected to match the readiness of the participants to deal with their own self-assessments, on the one hand, and with the objective problems found in the school, on the other.

There is no magic to these meetings. The components of

success consist of hard work and the dedication of faculty that permits critical self-examination, the first step in Human Relations training. It is not unusual for participants to confide with the trainers that the things learned about themselves in preparation for these meetings extend into the "non school" part of their lives. Some participants have confessed that the training made a pretty dull marriage into a much more interesting one. Other participants have said the experience has improved their relationships at home, with their parents, with their children and with friends. But this is not the intent of the Human Relations training. It focuses on the individual in the school setting. It simply appears to be the case that when a person engages in self-reflection for school purposes, benefits accrue in non-school activities as well.

The impact of the aspect of the training is felt most directly in the faculty-to-students relationships. Faculty members are helped to achieve better face-to-face interactions with students. This does not mean more permissive relationships, but more effective ones. The model is for faculty to try to help guide students toward discovering personal goals and then to assist the progress toward these goals. It can be easy for teachers to get caught in the trap of thinking that certain students should limit their goals; to be realistic about what they can achieve. While this might be appropriate in some cases, the general strategy in Human Relations Training is to focus on enhancing the options of students, rather than limiting them. By entertaining the maximum possibilities feasible for a student, the teacher may avoid the tragic error of obstructing talent. The problem, then, with expanding alternatives, becomes directing and encouraging behavior toward achieving successive levels of goals.

GROUP TRAINING

In addition to the sessions devoted to Individual training there are sessions in which the emphasis is on group training. These group sessions build upon the individual sessions, and serve to support them. While the emphasis is on the internal process in the individual training, the group training focuses on external, interpersonal aspects of the individual. Obviously, it is impossible to separate the two.

The group training is concerned with who does what at both the school level of organization, and the classroom level of organization. By focusing on the various roles in the school, faculty and trainers are in positions to examine the kinds of decisions that are made, and the values implicit on the decisions. The facilitator serves the purpose of maintaining the focus. When teachers and faculty are given this time to involve themselves in decisions, they begin to have an influence on the administration of the school. We find in these group training sessions that faculty often hear of outcomes, but rarely know the reasons behind the decision. The concern of faculty regarding the *reasons* for which decisions are made is clear. Such reasons serve as principles which become focal points for future decisions.

HUMAN RELATIONS TRAINING AND SCHOOL CRIME

Human Relations Training is not intended as a technique solely aimed at reducing school crime. However, a great deal of school crime results because of the institutionalized racism practiced in the school system. We view racism as contributory to crime.

Schools with racist policies, or clearly prejudicial faculty are often the targets for considerable vandalism, classroom control problems, and worse. Other direct results of racism and prejudiced behaviors by faculty members are absenteeism, academic indifference and low student body morale.

Indirect effects of racism and prejudice are more pervasive than direct ones, but are difficult to identify. Since racism and prejudice are invidious phenomena, their practice tends to result in lowered self-esteem in students. Students who are compared unfavorably with others because of ethnic membership, sex or physical handicap, come to resent the school and form "out groups" or collectives of similarly perceived persons for the purposes of self-support. Thus, the school which purposefully or accidentally shows discrimination policy *alienates* those who are the subject of discrimination and forces them to adopt clearly oppositional values and practices. Anti-school behaviors such as conspicuous use of drugs and grafitti become the way such "out group" members announce their independence from institutions which devalue them, and the anger and outrage shown by the school officials serve as sources of satisfaction by the out group members.

SUMMARY

Human Relations Training is a process of helping a faculty and administration become more aware of prejudices within themselves and of identifying policies and procedures which favor white males at the expense of all other groups. The training is specifically designed for this purpose and focuses, through an assessment procedure of interviews and questionnaires, on issues pertinent to the self-assessment of individuals on the one hand, and upon the operation of the social structure of the school operations on the other. The training is modeled after the instruction developed by the authors at the Human Relations Program, University of Minnesota, and Human Development, Ltd., Honolulu, Hawaii. As practiced by these institutions, Human Relations is not a programmed experience but one which is developed to meet the needs of each school which requests such training. The principles of the training consist of the assumption that individuals and systems in this country have been influenced by our racist history, and of the assumption that strong desire exists in many individuals to divest ourselves of the detrimental and unfair aspects of this heritage. The training may be conducted through blocked hours, may last for a few days, or for an extended period of time. It consists of a contract period, then of successive group meetings and decision making meetings, and a final evaluation involving training staff and school staff. The implications for school crime are considerable in some schools, and less in others.

DEFINITIONS

MINORITY: Any group that views itself and/or is defined by a dominant power elite as unique on the basis of perceived physical, cultural, economic, and/or behavioral characteristics and is treated accordingly in a negative manner.

PREJUDICE: "Hardening of the Categories" — An attitude, usually emotional, acquired in advance of adequate evidence and experience. It is based upon varying combinations of suggestion, imitation, belief, and limited experience and may be either favorable or unfavorable. Specific prejudices are forms of sympathy or antipathy and may have as their objects, individuals, groups, races, nationalities (or the particular traits of any one of these), or ideas, social patterns, and institutions.

RACISM: When an elite group (dominant) develops a social system in which race is the major criterion of role assignment, role rewards and socialization, and has the power to enforce those decisions.

INSTITUTIONAL RACISM: Institutional racism represents a social system in which race is the major criterion of role assignment, role rewards, and socialization. After colonial contact takes place, elite monopoly of political, economic, social, cultural, and psychological resources develops, resulting in a social system which is oppressive of all minorities.

DECENTRALIZATION RECONSIDERED:
SCHOOL CRIME PREVENTION THROUGH COMMUNITY INVOLVEMENT

William T. Pink
University of Nebraska

David E. Kapel
University of Nebraska

It is often argued that the problems of the public schools, including school-based violence and vandalism, could be dealt with most effectively by decentralizing the schools and involving the local community in the educational decision-making process. The theory is that decentralization, through community participation, will bring about a sense of community "ownership" of school problems as well as a collective responsibility for their solution. Yet in few school districts has decentralization actually led to community involvement in decision-making or to the collective responsibility for problem-solving presumed to accompany it. In most cases, school decentralization has been achieved by taking the city-wide political educational model down to the smaller decentralized unit — politics and business as usual but in a scaled-down setting (1).

The repeated failure of decentralization to actively involve the community in the operation of its schools or to mobilize community resources to deal with school problems should not be taken as an indication that decentralization cannot produce these and other desirable results. In districts where decentralization has been attempted or achieved, a majority of parents and other community residents continue to be excluded under the new system. Consequently, the schools and their problems do not come to be seen as belonging to the whole community and the school remains a hostile territory. What is needed, in conjunction with school decentralization, is a new model of school governance which disperses decision-making power throughout the community and draws into the educational system a truly representative group of those most affected by its policies and practices: the parents of children in school.

A NEW MODEL FOR SCHOOL GOVERNANCE

The model proposed here decentralizes educational decision-making to the smallest meaningful unit — the school building (2). Each school becomes the focal point of a decentralized "district" within the original parent school district. Since decentralization is taken to the school unit and a local decentralized school board makes policy only for its own school, board representatives and their constituency are brought closer together. Each community board, which has primary vested interest in a particular school, also is tangentially connected to the City-wide School Board through a Congress of Local Decentralized Boards serving in an advisory capacity (see Figure 1).

The heart of the proposed model is the local decentralized school board formed at the school building level. Each school would have its own board or, more appropriately, each school board would have its own school.The local board would be made up of 12 to 14 parents of children attending the school. There may be times when the school board will include some non-parents among their members (e.g., local businessmen might serve on boards of vocational schools), but three-fourths of the parents in the school would have to vote for such variation and non-parent members would be randomly selected from those nominated by parents. No more than 25 percent of each board should be made up of non-parents, since parents should remain the primary decision-makers.

For each school grade two parents would be randomly selected to sit on the school board. If a parent refused to serve, the next number would be selected. Random selection would insure that each parent would have equal opportunity to be selected for board membership (3). Since politics would not

147

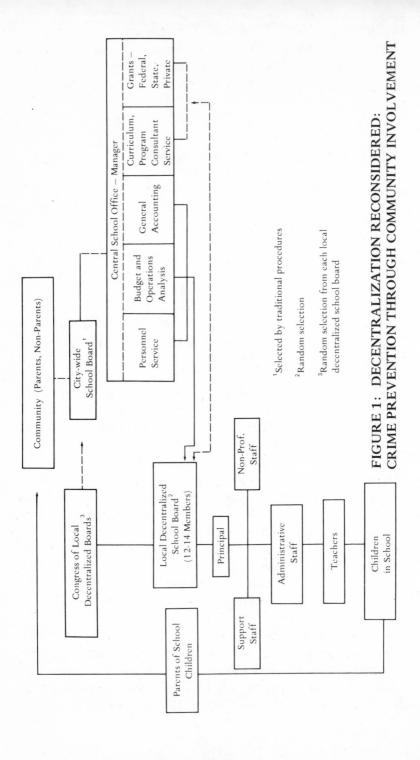

FIGURE 1: DECENTRALIZATION RECONSIDERED: CRIME PREVENTION THROUGH COMMUNITY INVOLVEMENT

Community (Parents, Non-Parents)

City-wide School Board[1]

Central School Office — Manager

Personnel Service

Budget and Operations Analysis

General Accounting

Curriculum, Program Consultant Service

Grants — Federal, State, Private

[1]Selected by traditional procedures

[2]Random selection

[3]Random selection from each local decentralized school board

Congress of Local Decentralized Boards[3]

Local Decentralized School Board[2] (12-14 Members)

Principal

Non-Prof. Staff

Administrative Staff

Teachers

Children in School

Support Staff

Parents of School Children

play a part in selection, becoming a member of the school board would not depend on individual political skills nor could special interest groups unduly influence the selection process. From the least to the most articulate, each parent, regardless of race, sex, or socioeconomic status, would have an equal chance of participating in the educational decision-making process.

At the secondary level there would be equal representation for each grade level. Members would serve three years (or as long as his or her child attended the school) and could be re-selected by the random procedure. To insure a degree of board stability across selection periods, no more than one-third of the board would be replaced each year. Recall procedures would be developed for each class level to remove members from local school boards. If 40 percent of the parents in a class petitioned and 80 percent voted for recall, then a new school representative would be randomly selected. Funding would be made available to pay employers for substitutes to replace board members (if regular release time is impossible), although most board business would be transacted during evening meetings. A small stipend also would be paid each board member for active participation in the business of the board.

Local decentralized school boards would have broad decision-making authority with respect to curricula and program policy, school philosophy, budget development (within guidelines set by the City-wide School Board), hiring, evaluation, and dismissal of staff (but not contract negotiation), use of resources available locally as well as those available through the Central Office, and development of all policies required by the school administration to meet the educational needs of the children and the community within its catchment area. The local board should be sensitive to the changing needs of the community and able to translate these needs into action when appropriate. There must be a proper mix of representative and leadership functions of the board.

The local school boards would be involved only in policy-making, not in the daily administration or operation of the school. School administration would remain the responsibility of the building principal. The principal's role, however, would become more like that of the school superintendent; that is, he or she would have much more administrative authority than currently is typical of school principals. Directly responsible only to the local decentralized school board, the school principal would be supported by both a professional and an administrative staff. These staffs would be responsible for creating a teaching/learning environment to meet the educational, psychological, and social needs of students within the broad policies established by the local boards.

School personnel would be asked to supply information needed by the board in making defensible policy decisions and to offer recommendations regarding special educational solutions (e.g., curriculum, methods, and materials). The school board, which would retain the right to question and/or reject the suggestions of school personnel, must at the same time respect and carefully consider their professional advice.

A Congress of Local Decentralized Boards would be formed by random selection of representatives from the local decentralized school boards. In large urban areas, a single representative from each school might be selected, while in smaller districts there may be two or more school representatives. The Congress would advise the City-wide School Board on local schools' needs with respect to budget development, personnel service, budget and operations analysis, general accounting, and grants. It also would provide a meeting place for local boards as well as an environment in which new city-wide approaches could be developed and examined. The Congress would be a source of new ideas and support for local boards, as well as a place for lobbying to influence the City-wide School Board.

The City-wide School Board, elected at large or by district, made up of parents, nonparents, businessmen, lawyers, etc. (i.e., those individuals who currently serve on school boards), would determine city taxes or other sources of school support, to insure adequate funding for all schools; establish an overall budget, including "block grants" to local decentralized boards;

protect and nurture the buying power of the entire school system; negotiate and let contracts with teachers and other personnel; and set policies and funding levels for the Central School Office.

The Central School Office would be headed by an educational manager who, in addition to administering this office, would develop a city-wide budget, act as staff consultant to both the City-wide School Board and local decentralized school boards, and function in the manner determined by City-wide School Board policies. This managerial position would be directly responsible only to the City-wide School Board with one exception — if 80 percent of the local decentralized boards voted to remove the manager for cause, the City-wide School Board would be obligated to replace him.

Staff of the Central School Office would offer advice and assistance to professional and nonprofessional staff at the local level on administrative procedures and policies, curriculum development, new programs, and other matters. Their decision-making and administrative authority would be limited to the allocation of funds for local budgets and final approval of the general budget within guidelines set by the City-wide School Board. All contracts would be negotiated and let through the Central School Office. All federal, state, and local grant funds, and the administrative forms and procedures associated with them, would be handled by this office, although local boards would both prepare proposals and manage the grants they received. Central Office would be available for consultation on grant proposals and would develop general accounting procedures and other administrative operations.

To provide these services, the Central School Office would be made up of five units (4). Three of these units (Personnel Service, Budget and Operations Analysis, and General Accounting) would have direct authority and supervisory functions, although the latter also would act in a consultant capacity. Two units (Curriculum and Program; and Grants) would be primarily consultative.

COMMUNITY INVOLVEMENT AND CRIME PREVENTION

The model for school governance proposed here remedies several flaws which marred earlier attempts to decentralize the schools. By design, it both depoliticizes the process of school board selection and more widely disperses educational decision-making power. As a result, a revitalization of community interest and involvement in the schools is achieved and problem ownership, a prerequisite to problem solution, is returned to the community attached to each school.

Active community involvement in educational decision-making through the local decentralized school board should contribute significantly to a reduction in school crime by making the school and its policies more responsive to the needs of the community it serves and by increasing both parent and student commitment to the school and school programs. Increased parental involvement in educational decision-making should lead initially to the widespread legitimation of the school as a vital community institution and subsequently to an active commitment to school programs and goals. Further, it is expected that as the community defines and meets its educational needs and objectives the school will come to be shaped in such a way that student commitment to their school also will increase and the incidence of antisocial behavior will decline.

While community revitalization through school decentralization may seem particularly appropriate for inner-city school districts (5), it would be a serious mistake to consider the proposed model for school governance less applicable to suburban or small-town communities. Educational problems, including school crime, know no socioeconomic boundaries and suburban parents have been underrepresented in the governance structure of their schools just as have their counterparts in the urban ghettos. Decentralization, through random selection of parents for school board membership, should be seen as a viable strategy for facilitating educational change in any community. Simplistically, it is suggested that the community, through broad-based representation at the school board level, will both design an educational program and create a social environment which will meet the needs of its students. This, in turn, should dramatically reduce the incidence of school crime and delinquency.

FOOTNOTES

1. On decentralization of schools in Detroit and in New York City, see: Fantini, M. and Gittell, M., DECENTRALIZATION: ACHIEVING REFORM (New York, Praeger, 1975); Maeroff, G., "Local board role still limited," NEW YORK TIMES, May 7, 1975; Ornstein, A., RACE AND POLITICS IN SCHOOL/COMMUNITY ORGANIZATIONS (Pacific Palisades, Goodyear, 1974); Schiff, M., "The educational failure of community control in inner-city New York," PHI DELTA KAPPAN, 57 (6): 1976; Shanas, B., "New York decentralization – a mixed bag," NEW YORK AFFAIRS, Summer/Fall, 1976. See also: Bauer, G., *et. al.* EIGHT EXPERIMENTS IN COMMUNITY CONTROL (Cambridge, Mass., Arthur D. Little, 1969); Fein, L. J., THE ECOLOGY OF THE PUBLIC SCHOOLS: AN INQUIRY INTO COMMUNITY CONTROL (New York: Pegasus, 1971); Goldberg, G., "Class action, community organization, and school reform," IRCD BULLETIN, 11 (2): 1-12, 1976; Greenblatt, S. L., "The community school: a case study in educational innovation," URBAN EDUCATION, 11 (4): 441-58, 1977; Hatton, B. R., "Schools and black community development," EDUCATION AND URBAN SOCIETY, 9 (2):215-233, 1977; Levin, H. M. (ed.), COMMUNITY CONTROL OF SCHOOLS (Washington, D.C., Brookings Institute, 1970); Ziegler, H. L. *et. al.*, GOVERNING AMERICAN SCHOOLS: POLITICAL INTERACTION IN LOCAL

SCHOOL DISTRICTS (North Scituate, Mass., Dux-
bury Press, 1974).

2. For a more detailed description of this model see: Kapel,
   D. and Pink, W., "The school board: Participatory
   democracy revisited," URBAN REVIEW, in press.

3. To guarantee representation of persons who constitute an
   extremely small minority a stratified random sampl-
   ing procedure should be employed to guarantee pro-
   portional representation of all subgroups in the building population.

4. The Central School Office staff would be small but of very
   high quality. Their primary concern would be provision of services to local boards and performance of
   staff functions for the City-wide School Board. Personnel service would deal exclusively with city-wide
   regulations, contract implementation, and general
   personnel and manpower needs. Budget and Operations
   Analysis would prepare budgets, disburse funds, and
   develop cost accounting procedures for use by local
   schools. General Accounting would supervise cash
   flow operations and consult on student accounting
   and support. Within this unit would be housed the
   Student Support specialists (e.g., psychologists, special
   education experts, reading and speech specialists, etc.)
   used to reinforce the specialists hired by the local
   boards. The Curriculum and Program Development
   unit would supply consultants to local boards on request. The Grants unit would offer consultation on
   location, writing, and follow-through of state, federal,
   and private funding proposals.

5. A study of school board membership in New York City
   cited by Fantini and Gittell (*op. cit. supra* note 1)
   showed that, in a public school system which is 57.2
   percent black and Puerto Rican, 63.8 percent of
   board members were middle class professionals, over
   50 percent were Catholic and 36 percent Jewish, and
   53.2 percent had children in parochial not public
   schools. This was following decentralization of the
   City's public schools.

THE HUMAN ECOLOGY OF SCHOOL CRIME:

A CASE FOR SMALL SCHOOLS

James Garbarino
Research Division
Boys Town
Center for the Study of Youth Development

The multiple sufficient conditions for school crime are dealt with in the vast literature exploring the dynamics of crime in general and juvenile delinquency in particular (1). The *necessary* condition for school crime, however, is a social climate that permits a perpetrator-victim relationship to be created and to persist (2). In attempting to prevent school crime our task is to identify the factors which bring about a school social climate conducive to crime and to alter these in an effort to produce a more desirable social climate within the school.

The crux of the matter, it seems, is the school's ability to function as a "support system," which, according to Caplan, works to offset deficiencies in communication within the larger society by providing individuals with feedback about themselves, validations of their expectations about others, and support in handling emotion and controlling impulses: "They tell him (the individual) what is expected of him and guide him in what to do. They watch what he does and they judge his performance" (3).

The structure, policies, and organization of a school significantly affect its ability to function as a support system. This fact may be demonstrated by examining the role of school size in shaping social climate. The example of school size illustrates the way in which social/structural factors lead to antisocial behavior because it shows how alienation, apathy, and

155

anomie (and their behavioral correlates) arise as psychological adaptation to a socially inadequate setting.

SCHOOL SIZE AND SOCIAL CLIMATE

Many investigators have examined the impact of size upon the social dynamics of the secondary school (4). McPartland and McDill, for example, reviewed some of the evidence relating school size to school crime, focusing on the mediating factor of "responsiveness" (defined in terms of access to governing decisions, the costs of misbehavior, and rewards for desired behavior). In their analysis a small but significant relationship was demonstrated favoring the small school (5). Plath also reported a case study of a school in which incidents of serious student misconduct declined from 120 to nine following subdivision of a large high school into a number of smaller schools (6). While these and other studies indicate that large schools are likely to experience more crime, some research has suggested why this may be so.

A number of studies have shown that large schools tend to discourage both student participation in social activities and a sense of responsibility and commitment to school, particularly among academically marginal students (7). Although large schools offer more settings in which students can participate, there are proportionally more students to fill those settings. The large school, for example, may have both a chorus and a glee club, but it still is more difficult to get into either than it is to be a part of the single vocal group of a smaller school. Students in larger high schools participate less frequently in school activities than do their counterparts in small schools and they participate in a more limited variety of activities and settings. Only a small elite group can be genuinely active and "needed" in a large school (8).

Unfortunately, the students who are likely to be excluded from activities in a large school are those who could benefit most by participation — marginal students who have difficulty academically, demonstrate lower I.Q.s, and come from lower socioeconomic backgrounds. For such students participation in school activities could provide an alternative to academic pursuits, giving them an opportunity to experience success and develop a sense of personal identity and a commitment to school.

> *Alternatives to academic performance give the pupil a chance to succeed in achievement oriented activities even though he may not be able to do well in the classroom. How these alternative activities differ from those of the classroom is as important as the fact that they do so differ, as evidenced by the case of athletics . . . either the rigors of competition and judgment characteristic of the classroom are mitigated, or the activity in question has its own built-in source of support and personal protection, not to the same extent as in the family, but more than is available in the crucible of the classroom* (9).

Exclusion from alternative school activities may elicit a self-protective severing of identification or allegiance, especially among marginal students with no other source of commitment to school. When large numbers of such students are excluded the result is likely to be a pervasive climate of irresponsibility in which school crime can and often does flourish. Large schools, then, by depriving "superfluous" students of important experiences in participatory roles, exert a negative influence on character development, retard effective socialization, and disrupt orderly social relations (10).

Another characteristic of large schools which negatively affects the school social climate is the tendency toward "universalistic" or impersonal rather than particularistic relationships. Getzels differentiates these two approaches:

> *Rights and obligations are determined on impersonal rather than personal grounds. In the particularistic relationship the important question is who is involved; in the universalistic relationship the important question is what is involved* (11).

Schools in general tend to be universalistic in that functional considerations are primary; but in small schools there also are tendencies in the opposite direction which offset the impersonal quality of most interactions.

It might be concluded that while small schools make reasonable demands on students to accommodate both universalistic and particularistic influences, large schools tend to be excessively universalistic and to treat students instrumentally (12). The large school understandably requires many rules and regulations in order to function smoothly, but students often resent the treatment they receive under such a system. In studying the adolescent experience of schooling, Buxton found:

> . . . *very strong attitudes among many students: They do not like being treated alike; they come close to despising the pass system; they would like more choice about what to study and when to study it; they think there are too many rules; they would like more decision-making power; they do not feel the school has to have such strict controls; and they are rather against schedules* (13).

As schools increase in size, student objections to strict controls, the lack of choice or decision-making power, and uniformity rather than individual attention are very likely to increase as well. As an adaptation to an unresponsive environment, many students (and staff) will become passive and uncommitted to school; others will react in anger or frustration. The marginal or unsuccessful student is particularly likely to experience the negative effects of the large school and, as increasing numbers of such students are compelled to remain in school, the likelihood of their "finding" one another and forming educationally and socially deviant peer groups also is enhanced.

School staff as well as students are affected by the negative aspects of large schools. As school size increases, administration becomes more centralized, bureaucratic, and inflexible. Staff relations are depersonalized and teachers may feel the need to organize as a militant interest group (14). Large educational

158

bureaucracies and the accompanying proliferation of rules also decrease innovation, responsiveness, and adaptation (15), a fact which has important implications for school crime. Controlling crime in the school requires not only a personalized social climate, but considerable flexibility and responsiveness to the need for change.

To recapitulate, large schools tend to promote alienation among students by depriving many of them of opportunities for participation in extracurricular activities which are vital in the peer-oriented social system of adolescents. This effect is aggravated for students who are academically marginal and, therefore, predisposed to alienation as a response to failure. Both students and staff also are alienated by the impersonal quality of relationships in the large school and the bureaucratic and inflexible nature of its administration.

LARGE SCHOOLS: AN ECOLOGICAL "CONSPIRACY"

The development of American educational institutions — and indeed all American institutions — has not operated under an assumption of high priority for smallness. There is a thrust toward bigness inherent in the life of Western societies (16) and "enrollments" in all institutions have been allowed to grow in a generally haphazard and unplanned manner. Little or no consideration has been given to the impact of growth upon social dynamics and even in cases where planning has been undertaken it has been in the direction of promoting largeness. This has been particularly true of schools as, throughout the country over the past few decades, small schools have disappeared in favor of large ones. But the unchecked growth of schools has been mirrored by similar developments in the rest of society.

The effect of the large school on students, then, is not the whole story since size appears as part of a broader ecological "conspiracy." A study by Blyth et al. (17) found that grade cohorts in junior high schools (grades 7 to 9) were uniformly and substantially larger than grade cohorts in extended elementary schools (kindergarten to grade 8). In the city they studied there was no overlap in the distribution of sizes between the two types of schools. Comparing seventh graders in both types of school, the level of victimization (including robbery, physical beating, and theft in or around school) was substantially higher in the junior high schools (42%) than in the K-8 schools (25%). Anomie was higher and participation lower among the junior high school seventh graders as well.

Not only do issues of school structure and school size tend to be confounded, but when school size and size of community coincide the negative effects of each tend to be reinforced. In both the school and the community, bigness implies an instrumental and impersonal orientation in interpersonal and institutional relationships. Such an orientation is likely to generate alienation in both settings, city and school. Barker and Gump note this parallelism in their research:

> *In general, the schools and communities were harmonious: the small communities, like the small schools, provided positions for functional importance for adolescents more frequently; and the large cities, like the large schools, provided such positions less frequently. The data provide no evidence that the urban environments of the large schools compensated by means of their greater resources and facilities for the relatively meager functional importance of students within their large schools* (18).

Working together, the large city and the large school form a consistent human ecology dominated by impersonal and instrumental interactions (19). Youthful alienation is generated in both systems and both not only permit but stimulate antisocial behavior.

But why are schools big? They could be small. One reason for their growth has been the educational emphasis on "cognitive" academic curricula and the accompanying interest in the power of large schools, their ability to provide diverse resources for the intellectual development of students (20). Concern for the social issues in the matter of school size has been lacking, apparently in the belief that the primary issues were "academic." This reasoning has been noted by Heath:

> Central to academic improvement was the belief that excellence required a major structural change in the size of the school. To provide comprehensive education that included diverse and specialized courses, better facilities, and guidance services, many states mandated the consolidation of small schools into large schools. In Pennsylvania, for example, small high schools of 400-600 students that unquestionably offered high-quality education were forced to merge to create high schools of several thousand students (21).

Another reason for the merging of small schools into large probably has been the belief in the cost-effectiveness of the larger school. The question of financial efficiency is foremost in the minds of many educational administrators. Yet small schools are a better psychological investment and they may be good financial investment as well. Turner and Thrasher reviewed the evidence bearing on the question: "What is the optimal size for high schools given financial efficiency, psychological development, and educational quality?" They concluded that there is a fiscally and psychologically optimal size beyond which the economic virtues of largeness are not significantly enhanced and the psychological costs are substantial. These investigators have proposed that the optimal size for a secondary school lies somewhere in the range of 700 to 1,000 students (22). Other investigators have argued for a smaller "optimal" size. Rosenberg, for example, suggests that within an optimal range of 400 to 500 both economic and psychological economies appear to be addressed (23).

There is a point at which schools become large and beyond which the damage to social climate appears to be relatively constant. This is crucial because much of the research on school size has assumed a simple linear effect, often including no genuinely small schools in the design, only relatively small ones. "Optimal size" addresses the question of financial efficiency but it also should consider social and psychological costs, especially as these are translated into financial costs by their effect on school crime. Any estimate of the optimal size of the secondary school should be adjusted to take into account the characteristics of the student population. As the academic marginality of students increases optimal school size decreases. As youthful alienation increases because of historical trends towards age segregation, stressful family relations, and disrupted socialization, the need for small schools increases. A proper accounting of the costs involved in the school size issue must now include the impact of size on school crime. If it can be documented that small schools can reduce vandalism, the need for security measures, or institutionalization of delinquent students, their fiscal attractiveness will be enhanced.

PREVENTION OF SCHOOL CRIME

School crime does not occur in a social vacuum. It is found in schools which have lost their sense of institutional self-control and in which the social climate fosters alienation and irresponsibility. As such, it is an indicator of the "social habitability" or the quality of life within the school and, indeed, in the larger society. Our individualistic, laissez-faire approach to social relations too often blinds us to the importance of creating and maintaining a social climate within our institutions which actively promotes prosocial behavior. Rather than seeing the problem as one of simply stopping school crime, we must attempt first to create a social climate in which school crime is unlikely to occur.

In planning for crime prevention in schools there are three key policy questions: (1) How can we organize schools to maximize social control, particularly where marginal students are concerned? (2) How can we generate and sustain a social climate in schools that serves to motivate students to perform prosocial behaviors and, in so doing, use the prosocial majority to control antisocial subgroups? And (3) how can schools be protected from victimization by persons not part of the schools themselves? The answer to all three of these questions is to be found in enhancing the role of the school as a prosocial support system; that is, by making schools more effective in providing personal observation and feedback, in contingently reinforcing behavior, and in offering genuine opportunities for participation. Only by systematic attention to the social climate produced by school structure, size, and goals can behavior which occurs in interpersonal relationships be effectively regulated. Only by strengthening the identity of students *within* a school can their support be enlisted in identifying and controlling the anti-social activities of "outsiders."

There is an alternative to schools in which crime can occur unchecked. However, that alternative requires some changes in our thinking about what is important in a school environment. The following four objectives reflect these needed changes and together form the outlines of a strategy for combatting school crime.

1. *Create situational demands for participation.* This is important if a sense of collective responsibility for what goes on in school is to develop. As has been learned from the general problem of crime control, law enforcement in a free society can be effective only when it has the indigenous support of the citizenry. The application to school crime is clear. Reinforcing responsibility in the student as "citizen" is particularly important for the marginal student, whose academic citizenship is always in question.

2. *Create a social climate which encourages personal observation, accountability, and feedback.* Just as there is no substitute for the "cop on the beat" in the community, there is no better way to prevent school crime than by facilitating the development of personal relationships between staff and students (24). Schools must begin to operate as "support systems" for students and staff (25).

3. *Strive for heterogeneity.* Heterogeneous settings encourage individualization and individuation. Individual responsibility is a key element in establishing a climate inhospitable to school

crime. Moreover, heterogeneity permits the use of peer groups for prosocial ends where the social balance favors prosocial attitudes and behaviors (26).

4. *Arrange contingencies to reinforce prosocial behavior.* Where are the rewards in the school as a social system? Are they for individual or collective success? Are they for "keeping one's nose clean" or for being one's brother's keeper? Is good citizenship positively rewarded? It should be.

These four goals imply a need for systematic assessment of the school as a social system. At the same time they suggest a need for small schools since their attainment clearly is more feasible in the small school. The human ecology of school crime is dominated by two complementary forces — the depersonalization of the school through excessive size (27) and a general pattern of inadequate social identity (28). While the school can do relatively little to combat the more general social problem of alienation, by attending to issues of size and structure it can return a significant measure of control to prosocial forces within the school. Small schools emphasizing the creation and maintenance of enduring personalized social networks among students and staff offer considerable promise for the prevention and control of school crime.

FOOTNOTES

1. The school itself can be one of those sufficient conditions when it stimulates aggression, frustration and hostility.
2. The distinction between necessary and sufficient conditions is critical to both comprehension and intervention. See Bronfenbrenner, U. and Mahoney, M., "The structure and verification of hypotheses," In Bronfenbrenner, U. and Mahoney, M. (eds.) INFLUENCES

ON HUMAN DEVELOPMENT (Hinsdale, Ill.:Dryden, 1975); and Garbarino, J. "The human ecology of child maltreatment: a conceptual model for research," JOURNAL OF MARRIAGE AND THE FAMILY, in press.

3. The concept of the support system has been developed and elaborated by several investigators, among them Gerald Caplan. See Caplan, G., SUPPORT SYSTEMS AND COMMUNITY MENTAL HEALTH (New York: Grune & Stratton, 1976).

4. A recent literature search identified 344 articles pertaining to the topic of school size published in the last 15 years.

5. McPartland, J. and McDill, E., THE UNIQUE ROLE OF SCHOOLS IN THE CAUSES OF YOUTHFUL CRIME (Baltimore: Johns Hopkins University, 1976).

6. Plath, K., SCHOOLS WITHIN SCHOOLS: A STUDY OF HIGH SCHOOL ORGANIZATION (New York: Bureau of Publications, Teachers College, Columbia University, 1965). Alternative explanations of the reduction in misconduct must be entertained, of course, including the bugaboo of educational innovation, the "Hawthorne effect."

7. Baird, L., "Big school, small school: A critical examination of the hypothesis," JOURNAL OF EDUCATIONAL PSYCHOLOGY, 60: 253-60, 1969; Barker, G. and Gump, V. BIG SCHOOL, SMALL SCHOOL; HIGH SCHOOL SIZE AND STUDENT BEHAVIOR (Stanford, Calif.: Stanford University Press, 1964); Grabe, M. "Big school, small school: impact of the high school environment," Paper presented at the Annual Meeting of the American Educational Research Association, Washington, D.C., March, 1975; Wicker, A. "Cognitive complexity, school size and participation in school behavior settings: A test of the frequency of interaction hypothesis," JOURNAL OF EDUCATIONAL PSYCHOLOGY, 60: 200-203, 1969.

8. Barker, G. and Gump, V., *supra* note 7.

9. Dreeben, R., ON WHAT IS LEARNED IN SCHOOL

(Reading, Mass.: Addison-Wesley, 1968), pp. 72-3.

10. Garbarino, J., "The role of schools in socialization to adulthood," EDUCATIONAL FORUM, in press. Garbarino, J. and Bronfenbrenner, U., "The socialization of moral judgment and behavior in cross-cultural perspective," in Lickona, T., (ed.), MORAL DEVELOPMENT AND BEHAVIOR (New York: Holt, Rinehart and Winston, 1976).

11. Getzels, J. W., "Socialization and education: A note on discontinuities," TEACHER'S COLLEGE RECORD, (76), 218-225, 1974. See p. 223.

12. Burns, M. "The case for small schools," Paper presented to the Minnesota Interim Commission on Education, April, 1968.

13. Buxton, C. E., ADOLESCENTS IN SCHOOL (New Haven, Yale University Press, 1973), pp. 113-14. See also Blyth, D., Simmons, R., and Bush, D. "The transition into early adolescence: a longitudinal comparison of children in two educational contexts," Paper presented to the Biennial Meeting of the Society for Research in Child Development, New Orleans, March 17-20, 1977.

14. Coleman, J. S., et. al., YOUTH: TRANSITION TO ADULTHOOD (Chicago: University of Chicago Press, 1974).

15. Averch, H. et. al. HOW EFFECTIVE IS SCHOOLING? A CRITICAL REVIEW OF RESEARCH (Englewood Cliffs, N.J.: Educational Technology Publications, 1974), pp. 105, 173. See also, A FOUNDATION GOES TO SCHOOL (New York: Ford Foundation, 1972).

16. Schumacher, E. F., SMALL IS BEAUTIFUL: ECONOMICS AS IF PEOPLE MATTERED (New York: Harper and Row, 1973).

17. Blyth, et. al., supra note 13.

18. Barker and Gump, supra note 7.

19. Barker and Schoggen, QUALITIES OF COMMUNITY LIFE (San Francisco: Jossey-Bass, 1973).

20. Conant, J. B., THE AMERICAN HIGH SCHOOL TODAY: A FIRST REPORT TO INTERESTED CITIZENS (New York: McGraw-Hill, 1959); Jackson, J. L.

SCHOOL SIZE AND PROGRAM QUALITY IN SOUTHERN HIGH SCHOOLS (Nashville, Tenn.: Center for Southern Education Studies, George Peabody College for Teachers, 1966).

21. Heath, D. H., "Student alienation and school," SCHOOL REVIEW, (78): 51-528, 1970.

22. Turner, C. and Thrasher, M., SCHOOL SIZE DOES MAKE A DIFFERENCE (San Diego: Institute for Educational Management, 1970).

23. Rosenberg, N., "School size as a factor in school expenditure," JOURNAL OF SECONDARY EDUCATION, (45): 135-142, 1970.

24. Moos, R., "Evaluating and changing community settings," AMERICAN JOURNAL OF COMMUNITY PSYCHOLOGY, (4): 313-326, 1976.

25. Caplan, *supra* note 3.

26. Feldman, R. A., THE ST. LOUIS EXPERIMENT: GROUP INTEGRATION AND BEHAVIORAL CHANGE, NIMH Center for Studies of Crime and Delinquency Research Report Series (Washington, D.C.: U.S. Government Printing Office, 1974).

27. Garbarino, J. "High school size and adolescent social development," HUMAN ECOLOGY FORUM, 1973, 4, 26-29.

28. Bronfenbrenner, U., "The origins of alienation," in Bronfenbrenner, U., and Mahoney, M. (eds.) INFLUENCES ON HUMAN DEVELOPMENT (Hinsdale, Ill.: Dryden, 1975.

NEGOTIATING SCHOOL CONFLICT TO PREVENT
STUDENT DELINQUENCY

John De Cecco
John Roberts
San Francisco State University

In much of the current literature on school crime (1), school conflict and student delinquency are referred to synonomously; yet the two are clearly distinguishable and, while school conflict probably is inevitable, student delinquency surely is not. Delinquent behavior, which often results from the way in which the school deals with conflict, can be prevented by employing the techniques of negotiation in resolving school conflict.

Unfortunately, teachers and school officials typically use one of two main strategies in dealing with student delinquency: avoidance or force. The first represents a denial by school personnel that serious conflict with students exists. In the classroom this may take the form of ignoring student tardiness, absenteeism, or disruption of classes and even ignoring the failure to teach or to learn. Delinquent conduct in halls or restrooms and on school grounds also may be overlooked in an attempt to avoid the issue, while tensions within the school may be blamed on outsiders or on racial, socioeconomic, or political pressures over which school personnel have no control.

When avoidance fails to prevent delinquency, the school may resort to the use of institutional force. Teachers assign school work as punishment, humiliate students in front of their peers or banish them from class and, occasionally, refuse to teach. School officials restrict student movement by closing the campus, denying work permits, constructing rigid class schedules, and suspending or expelling recalcitrant students. Both teachers and school officials also use institutional force when they detain students or use physical threat or attack. The use of institutional force, however, can escalate rather than reduce conflict (2). The following incident, as described by a student, illustrates this possibility:

"When I was 15, one day while walking in the corridors going to class I crossed the senior garden. I was pushed and then punched, then when I was finally pushed out I was seized by the school officials and taken to the office. While I was in the office, the principal scolded me for crossing the garden and threatened to suspend me. I also threatened the senior that pushed me. The principal threatened that if I should lay a hand on the student I would be expelled. He could have at least interrogated the other student but instead he released him almost immediately."

In another case, a student describes how the use of police in his school escalated anger in a conflict situation:

"Right now a "crisis" is happening in our school. All of a sudden the police just came into our school and now our school is loaded with policemen, who, for absolutely no reason at all, are insulting and mistreating the students. It seems that the students that have a free period during school have a big problem. If they leave school, they are called cutting. If they stay in the lobby they are kicked out of school, and if they stay out in front of the school, they are eligible to be arrested for "loitering." Yesterday, my sister was cursed at and shoved around by a policeman for standing on the side of the school. Today the students had a strike. I really wanted to go, but having a 7th period

I would have been called cutting, and I can't afford to have a bad record . . . The police have us damn mad and our hate will burst out of us soon (3)."

As these examples suggest, the use of force initially may decrease the incidence of delinquent acts, but it also is likely to increase anger which may produce even more delinquent and acting-out behavior in the long run.

SCHOOL CONFLICT AND DELINQUENCY

Three obvious sources of conflict are found in almost every school. First, during the period of adolescence young people develop their individuality. This requires them to experiment with and define their relationships to authority (in this case the school) which generally involves challenging authority to some extent. The school, on the other hand, is responsible for socializing its students, or teaching them cultural rules, roles, and obligations, which requires that school personnel exercise some authority over students. Not infrequently, therefore, the school's responsibility to exercise authority over students comes into direct conflict with students' needs to challenge that authority.

A second source of conflict stems from social differences existing within the typical school. Students' families usually vary in ethnic, racial, and religious background, socioeconomic status, and political inclination and influence. Minority students, in particular, may differ substantially from school personnel in these areas. Conflicts arise when either students or school personnel try to impose their lifestyles and values on other groups or individuals.

A third source of conflict arises from the continual student turnover as new students enter the school and others leave. Resolutions of conflicts which were agreeable to departing students may be totally unacceptable to entering students. Conflict resolution, therefore, is an ongoing process requiring constant attention to newly identified needs and concerns.

A major reason why students often resort to delinquent behavior in response to conflict is the lack of opportunity in school for students to express anger or verbalize their grievances in a manner which is considered legitimate. According to a "hydraulic" model of emotional expression, anger which is not expressed verbally in one situation is likely to be expressed physically in another. Student anger which cannot be expressed verbally in the classroom or in meetings with school personnel may, by displacement, take the form of delinquent or destructive behavior such as physical attacks on teachers or on other students or destruction of school property. Direct verbal expression of anger by students generally is discouraged when school personnel use avoidance and force. Student grievances, when these are verbally expressed, often are ignored or labelled by school personnel as improper or disrespectful of authority. When expression of anger is blocked in this way, students are likely to displace anger in acts of school delinquency which the school, in turn, ignores or punishes, thus escalating anger and conflict and increasing the likelihood of further delinquency.

Another reason why school conflict may generate delinquent behavior is the lack of opportunities in school for students to hear grievances stated by both parties to a conflict. Research on "de-centering" indicates that adolescents are capable of learning to view conflicts from another's point of view as well as from their own (4). To develop this ability to de-center, however, students must be given an opportunity to express their own grievances as well as to listen to those of others. When the school fails to provide such an opportunity for direct exchange of views, students are left with the notion that their side of any conflict is "right" and thus that their behavior, although delinquent, is justified.

A third reason why delinquent behavior may result from school conflict is the lack of opportunity for students to participate in decision-making which affects their own interests and welfare. In order to teach democratic principles and concern for others, the school must provide opportunities for students to recognize and demonstrate respect for civil liberties, including the rights to dissent, procedural and substantive due process, equality, and privacy, among others. A study of over 6,000 students in the New York, Philadelphia, and San Francisco metropolitan areas showed that students are able to identify the particular civil liberties at stake in school conflicts they experience (5). When the school does not provide opportunities for students to recognize and protect civil liberties, students may rightly view the school as an authoritarian and lawless institution in which the views, values, and interests of the more influential are imposed on less influential individuals and groups.

Much student delinquency results from the lack of opportunities to resolve conflicts in a rational manner. By ignoring the reasons for delinquent behavior, while simultaneously punishing it, the school only escalates anger, polarizes the issues, and generates a need for more avoidance or force to resolve conflicts or control delinquent behavior in the future.

A MODEL FOR SCHOOL NEGOTIATION

As an alternative to the use of avoidance or force in controlling conflict and delinquency, schools can institute a negotiation procedure which is designed to resolve conflict without increasing school delinquency. The principles of constructive negotiation between conflicting parties in school settings are outlined briefly below (6).

1. *Both parties should be given an opportunity for direct verbal expression of anger over specific issues.* This requires that the parties confront each other face-to-face, use the appropriate language and level of emotional expressions for verbalizing anger, and state issues in terms of the incidents which are believed to have precipitated the conflict.

2. *Both parties should analyze the conflict in terms of the issues as stated by each party and the possible or alleged violation of each party's civil liberties.* Each party should identify the civil liberties which may have been violated and the issues as they perceive them. The opportunity to express not only the cognitive

172

but also the emotional elements of a conflict enables both sides to assert more rational control over their own behavior.

3. *Both parties should agree to common statements of the issues.* Each party should establish the priority of its issues if there is more than one issue involved. Both should limit negotiation to specific issues contained in their jointly written statements. Statements must be written jointly by both parties since the act of agreeing on the wording of the issues provides an initial opportunity to move from confrontation to negotiation. By taking this step both parties recognize that, although they disagree, they can negotiate.

4. *Both parties should agree to gains and concessions for each side.* Each party should list its proposed resolutions, identify the gains and losses for each party and for each proposal, and rank the proposals so that critical gains are clearly indicated. On the basis of this information the parties can initiate bargaining and ultimately arrive at compromises acceptable to both sides.

5. *Both parties should agree to the allocation of responsibilities for implementing agreements.* This requirement, which provides for agreement by each party to mutual responsibilities, involves the assignment of tasks to each party, a determination of times when tasks are to be completed, and a determination of actions which can be taken by the other party if the responsible party fails to complete the assigned tasks.

6. *Both parties should agree to the conditions for evaluating implementation of agreements.* Both parties should agree on the times, places, and criteria for evaluating the success of implementation. This important requirement provides an opportunity for future negotiation of issues still unresolved or of new issues which subsequently arise (7).

THE NEGOTIATION MODEL IN ACTION

In an eighth-grade home economics class a conflict situation developed which was resolved effectively by the teacher and her students in a manner which illustrates the negotiation model in action. The class, which met twice a week (on Tuesdays and Thursdays), had been getting progressively more difficult to handle on Thursday afternoons. The teacher, who was desperately seeking relief from this problem, had the following to say about its resolution:

"... One Tuesday I told them something was happening to me on Thursdays that was getting to my family. I was actually too tired on Thursdays to cook dinner. I asked them if they could help me figure out a solution to the problem of the way I felt on Thursdays. Then I said, 'Part of the puzzle is why you get right down to work on Tuesdays and on Thursdays it takes half the period for you settle down. So we don't have much time for our class activities.'

They said that right after lunch they went directly to art class and that the art teacher would not let them talk for that 90-minute period. Then they went directly to home economics. They said, 'We've got to talk sometime.'

I did not allow any put-down of the art teacher by placing the blame on her. I said, 'You've told me your problem. Let me tell you mine. I come early to school on Thursday mornings for faculty meeting. I have no prep period on Thursdays. And my lunch hour is for playground duty on Thursdays. When you come in so noisily at the end of the day I actually develop a headache. I am beaten by the time I get home. What can I do?'

I wrote their suggestions on the chalkboard. One student suggested that I go to bed early on Wednesdays. Another suggested that I trade playground duty with another teacher on Thursdays. Another that I ask my family to help cook dinner on Thursdays.

I said, 'I promise I will follow your suggestions. If I give you five minutes at the beginning of class to let off steam, *do you think we could settle down to business?'*

They said they would try it. We agreed to try it for a week and then discuss it. We did try it and it worked for the rest of the semester. My classroom was next to the library in an old building with thick walls. I had to explain to the librarian before we allowed it to happen. When they came into the room they could let out as much noise as they wanted. As long as they knew they could do this for five minutes, they got more and more quiet. Talking replaced yelling after a while"(8).

This rather simple example of conflict resolution between students and their teacher follows the general requirements of the negotiation model. The students acknowledged that they needed to talk and let off steam. The teacher explained that she needed to get the class underway without excessive disruption and delay. Both parties expressed their anger somewhat indirectly: the students blamed the art teacher and the home economics teacher disguised her anger as helplessness. Both, however, also agreed on the issues, arrived at a set of mutually acceptable concessions, and devised a plan for implementation, including an agreed-upon time to evaluate the new arrangement.

More complicated conflict situations will require even closer attention to the details of negotiation and strict adherence to its principles. But, in either case, use of the negotiation model can prevent delinquency and reduce school conflict by providing opportunities for constructive resolution of disagreements. By providing for the direct verbal expression of anger the model reduces the necessity for students to displace anger onto innocent victims or to express it in violent and destructive behavior. By identifying and respecting students' rights, it teaches respects for the rights of others. And by offering an alternative to the self-defeating use of avoidance or force, the model enables school personnel and students to deal with conflict in ways that encourage democratic behavior and, in many instances, interrupt the vicious cycle of school conflict and delinquency.

FOOTNOTES

1. De Cecco, J. P. and Richards, A. K., "Civil war in the high schools: A cease-fire proposal," PYSCHOLOGY TODAY (Nov.):51-56, 120, 1975.
2. De Cecco, J. P. and Richards, A. K., GROWING PAINS: USES OF SCHOOL CONFLICT (New York: Aberdeen Press, 1974), p. 124.
3. *Ibid.*, pp. 118-119.
4. *Ibid.*
5. *Ibid.*
6. *Ibid.*
7. The authors gratefully acknowledge the help of James Rudolph in analyzing each step of the model.
8. De Cecco, J. P. and Richards, A. K., "Using negotiation for teaching civil liberties and avoiding liability," PHI DELTA KAPPAN, 57 (1):23-27, 1975.

TRAINING SPECIALISTS TO WORK
WITH DISRUPTIVE STUDENTS:

RATIONALE AND MODELS

Raymond Bell and Elizabeth Semmel
Lehigh University

Dealing with disruptive students in the classroom is made more difficult by controversies not only over methods but also with regard to responsibilities: Should parents be expected to handle their own children if their behavior causes problems for teachers and other students? Or is the school administrator ultimately responsible for a smoothly functioning school? Should the administrator "troubleshoot" for classroom teachers in order that they may get on with their educational tasks? Or, alternately, can the teacher, with special training and preparation, deal directly and immediately with disruptive or delinquent youth in their own classrooms? Research has indicated that the school, and the individual teacher in particular, may contribute to the generation of delinquent or disruptive behavior; this suggests that both also may play an important role in its prevention.

THE SCHOOL'S ROLE IN PREVENTION

There are important reasons for developing a delinquency treatment and prevention program which is based in the school as opposed to the community. Research on delinquency has suggested a critical role for the school in both causation and prevention (1). Poor school performance, for instance, is closely related to delinquency. Although this relationship is strongest for offenders of lower socioeconomic status, the chances of delinquency among youth from white-collar homes also increases with school failure (2). Repeated failure in school often results in a "failure" identity which can become chronic, leading to antisocial pathways in an attempt to preserve identity (3).

> A significant number of individuals continually receive punishments rather than rewards at report card time . . . Report cards as they are presently administered in most public schools have created a group of students who are the "perpetual losers," deprived of any taste of the academic honors that are the major official rewards in schools (4).

Delinquent and disruptive behavior, it seems, may be a method of dealing with the loss of self-esteem and the social stigma which are consequences of school failure (5).

Not only can the school contribute to delinquency, but it is within the school setting that early detection and effective prevention can begin. Failure, more visible within the school than almost anywhere else, starts early and is detectible even in kindergarten. Adolescents spend a significant amount of their waking hours in school and are most accessible in this setting. In addition, delinquent and disruptive acts often are perpetrated against the school in acts of "vindication and symbolic vandalism" (6). Neither public nor private agencies have had so much success in dealing with the problem of juvenile delinquency. Private agencies generally have chosen to work exclusively, or at least disproportionately, with a middle-class clientele (7). If an effective intervention program is not introduced within the school system, continuation of the pattern of growing disruption in both the schools and the community probably can be expected.

THE TEACHER'S ROLE IN PREVENTION

Research suggests that certain teachers consistently experience disruption in their classrooms, while others rarely have difficulty even with youth known to be "troublesome." In the latter case, a sense of mutual affection and trust between student and teacher generally is evident, with the teacher expressing genuine interest in these normally disruptive youth.

As one researcher posits, "students behave according to what they perceive to be their role. If they are expected to be subservient or inferior, they will behave accordingly, but they will ultimately rebel." (8). A classic study also has shown that teachers' attitudes can effect a significant increase in I.Q. scores when they are "misinformed" that the students have great potential (9). Conversely, a negative perception of delinquents by teachers has resulted in acceptance of a deviant role (10).

Studies also have revealed that most teachers, including those from backgrounds similar to their students', view disadvantaged students as "lazy" and "unmotivated" (11). Because delinquency so often coincides with a disadvantaged background there is a need for increasing the teacher's awareness of subcultural attitudes toward learning and of the learning ability of minority group students. Teachers must be trained to deal constructively with students who lack certain skills because of their subcultural membership.

Changes in teacher responses and attitudes also are needed if alienated and delinquent youth are to be handled effectively in the classroom. Frequently recommended are empathetic teaching approaches which help the teacher to see the learning situation through the eyes of the student and to become aware of the student's life situation outside the school setting. As Glasser has stated, "teachers have to get involved with students; it's critical for the whole procedure. Teachers have to care for children, and they have to show that they care" (12). Curriculum modifications to meet the special needs of "problem" students and capitalizing on strengths rather than reinforcing weaknesses also have been suggested (13).

Traditional teacher training systems clearly have been less than successful in preparing educators to deal successfully with delinquent populations. Most teachers lack the diagnostic and remedial teaching skills necessary to cope with the learning disabilities often associated with acting-out behavior. Nor have teachers been equipped with the crisis-intervention skills which help to defuse the hostility and anxiety underlying disruptive behavior. The two models presented here are designed to identify and train school personnel to implement intervention and prevention programs while increasing the academic skills of disruptive youth.

CHARACTERISTICS OF TEACHER TRAINING MODELS

The most effective teacher training programs, both in-service and pre-service, are characterized by the following hallmarks: teacher trainees are self-selected; the program is action-oriented; the competencies presented are viewed as necessary; and training is pragmatic, dealing with actual cases and, where possible, real situations. Assessment of the needs of the client population indicates that training should be offered in three general areas: diagnostic and remedial skills; crisis-intervention skills; and community-contact skills.

Since a significant proportion of delinquent and disruptive children and youth have learning disabilities which impede their acquisition of basic reading and arithmetic skills (14), many of these students are alienated from, and in conflict with, schools as institutions, teachers as helping agents, and education as a viable goal. The teacher, then, must have the ability to diagnose (in the radical sense, i.e., to know thoroughly) the nature of the learning disability, particularly as it relates to reading and math, and to develop and implement prescriptions to remedy the problem.

Both low self-esteem and the decision-making processes which lead to conflict with teachers, school and community must be dealt with simultaneously, often before the learning deficiencies can be addressed. Redl urges the use of crisis-intervention in the schools for the purpose of assessing and intervening in problem situations (15). According to Redl, "good education is not enough for children who hate . . . their basic ego disturbances must be repaired first (16)." Since the emotional content of most disruptive behavior must be dealt with firmly and purposefully, crisis-intervention skills should be developed as part of the training model.

180

The terms of reference and value structure of the disruptive youth originate in the community in which he lives. The family, the school, the peer group, and a variety of social agencies and institutions are forces which affect him and with which he comes into conflict. In order to deal effectively with the problems of such youth the teacher must have a realistic knowledge of both the formal and informal structures in the local community, including the political power structure and personalities involved. Acquisition of such knowledge – an essential part of the teacher's role as youth "advocate" – requires direct contact with these community influences.

These three areas of concern – diagnosis and remedial education, crisis intervention, and community contact – are not independent, nor are they mutually exclusive. Specific training objectives deriving from these areas can be described as follows:

First, the teacher shall be trained to develop a working knowledge of educational and achievement patterns of identified delinquent and disruptive populations; social and cultural forces which influence the self-concepts of alienated and delinquent youth; and informal and formal academic, social and psychological assessment techniques for identifying this population's needs.

Second, the teacher shall be trained to develop a personalized intervention plan in conjunction with the student for the purpose of preventing antisocial behavior. The teacher must develop a working knowledge of the public school system, the juvenile justice system, and social agencies and institutions in the community. The teacher also must learn to serve in an advocacy role to provide students with continuity in helping services, to contribute to the coordination of the efforts of varied agencies for the purpose of rehabilitation, and, when appropriate, to maintain ongoing communication with significant others in students' lives.

And third, the teacher shall be prepared to coordinate appropriate remediation through direct intervention, referral, or a combination of these.

These three objectives require that the teacher have a thorough understanding of: (1) the types of learning disability which are likely to retard learning; (2) teaching strategies (including both their implementation and evaluation) designed to increase basic reading and arithmetic skills of students who are educationally disadvantaged in these areas; (3) the fundamentals of curriculum construction, including individualized instruction and the selection of curriculum materials to enhance the student's self-image; (4) the types of behavior and attitude considered developmental and/or dysfunctional in adolescents; (5) the social forces which encourage or support delinquent and antisocial behavior; (6) the criminal justice system and its component parts (police, probation, courts); and (7) the rationales and techniques for counseling delinquent populations.

Two models which address these objectives by preparing teachers to manage disruptive youth while increasing their academic skills are presented below.

PRE-SERVICE MODEL FOR CRISIS-INTERVENTION

This model consists of an intensive training program at the graduate level conducted by an institute of higher education in cooperation with local school districts in which significant numbers of disruptive youth can be identified. It is suggested that a professional credential be awarded to those who successfully complete the training program. The recommended 15-month program would include three phases: pre-service, in-service, and terminal phase.

In the 16-week pre-service phase teacher trainees would spend half of each working day with other teachers identified as effective in "turning on" the "turned-off" youth. Here they would develop diagnostic, remedial, and crisis-intervention competencies under the supervision of the teacher and a specialist from the university. In the late afternoon and evening their time would be spent working in community centers and juvenile justice agencies (police departments, probation offices, or detention facilities). In the afternoons trainees also would meet with university instructors to discuss on-the-job experiences and problems. Much of this time should be spent in role-playing, case study, problem-solving, and developing diagnostic and remedial skills. Resource people may be used, including probation officers, street workers, inmates, drug counselors, addicts, juvenile court judges, institutional administrators, and other teachers. Visits to court, juvenile correctional facilities or drug centers also would be included. Emphasis would be placed on the development of diagnostic, remedial, and crisis-intervention skills.

The second phase — the core of the program — would be a one-year teaching internship in a selected school setting. During this time trainees would be visited at least twice a week by university staff with expertise in diagnostic and remedial teaching, curriculum and crisis-intervention. Seminars and tutorials dealing with solutions to specific problems could be held on-site rather than at the university.

The third and final phase of the program would consist of a 12-week integrating experience on campus where the interns meet to evaluate both the program and their experiences and to add some theoretical structure to the practical experience of their internship.

Teacher trainees should be selected on the basis of emotional stability, flexibility, and commitment to youth, and to cover a broad range of social and academic backgrounds. Both the pre-service component and the field placement should be rigorous, involving an investment of 60 hours a week. The in-service placement should expose trainees to potentially traumatic, threatening, and emotionally draining experiences. A major strength of the program design is the evolving group sense which can be developed by regular social gatherings in conjunction with seminar meetings and shared pre-service experiences. These experiences should be continued throughout the in-service phase despite any geographical distance separating trainees' respective job sites.

Instructional personnel for the program might be drawn from a wide range of professional backgrounds depending upon their availability. Areas of expertise may include: Social and Emotional Disturbance, Learning Disabilities, Curriculum Design, Law Enforcement and Corrections, Urban Problems, Community Relations, among many others.

IN-SERVICE MODEL FOR LOCAL SCHOOL SYSTEMS

The in-service model, while less ambitious than the pre-service model, may hold greater attraction for school administrators because it is cheaper and involves already employed personnel. This model, however, is more limited in scope and, while it deals with the same general competencies, it obviously will not produce specialists as highly trained as will the pre-service model.

It is suggested that three to five "target" school districts be identified by the State Education Agency. In each of these districts a cadre of ten to 15 teachers should be selected for their affinity for or skills in dealing non-punitively with disruptive youth. The in-service training program should be explained to these individuals who then should be given the option of enrolling on a volunteer basis.

The suggested model is ten months in length. In-service seminars in the areas of diagnostic and remedial teaching, learning disabilities, and crisis-intervention would be held on a weekly basis. If after-school time is required, appropriate compensation should be allocated. The in-service instructors should be available to act as consultant resource personnel. The cadre of teachers would be assigned a caseload, which should rarely exceed 20 students, identified by commonly accepted and clearly defined procedures. These students would be helped in any way deemed appropriate by the teacher to whom they are assigned. It is suggested that this model be coordinated with, and parallel to, programs for disruptive students developed by other consultants.

The two training models briefly presented here would have several important areas of impact. In addition to creating a new professional specialty and credential, the pre-service model would encourage the development of new programs leading to professional level work. Each model also fosters a recognition of the widening sphere of influence of the school in the community, as well as a better understanding of the work of the educator by other agencies which deal with disruptive youth. Increased contact between the school and other community agencies is widely regarded as desirable in any effort to reduce student delinquency.

The 1970 Joint Commission on Mental Health of Children urged that teacher training be restructured " . . . to deal with the wide range of behavior in children so that more can be maintained in the classroom (17)." In both of the proposed teacher training models the traditional teaching role would be expanded to provide assistance to students who traditionally have been ignored or pressured out of the school situation.

FOOTNOTES

1. Polk, K. and Schafer, W.E., SCHOOLS AND DELINQUENCY (Englewood Cliffs, N.J.: Prentice-Hall, 1972); Wenk, E.A., "Schools and delinquency prevention," in CRIME AND DELINQUENCY LITERATURE, June, 1974.
2. Winslow, R.W., JUVENILE DELINQUENCY IN A FREE SOCIETY (Encino, Cal.: Dickenson, 1968), p. 90.
3. Glasser, W., THE EFFECT OF SCHOOL FAILURE ON THE LIFE OF A CHILD (Washington, D.C.: National

Association of Elementary School Principals, 1971).

4. McPartland, J.M. and McDill, E.L., "Research on crime in the schools," Unpublished paper, Center for Social Organization of Schools, Johns Hopkins University, 1975, p. 17.

5. Elliot, D.S. and Voss, H.L., DELINQUENCY AND DROP-OUT (Lexington, Mass.: D.C. Heath, 1974).

6. Goldmeier, H., "Vandalism: the effects of unmanageable confrontation," ADOLESCENCE, 9:49-56, 1974.

7. Locke, H.G., Testimony before the United States Sub-Committe to Investigate Juvenile Delinquency, Washington, D.C., June 27, 1972.

8. Hilmar, W., "Attitudes toward and of disadvantaged students," ADOLESCENCE, 7:435-446, 1972, p. 437.

9. Rosenthal, R. and Jacobson, L., "Teachers' expectancies: determinants of pupils' I.Q. gains," PSYCHOLOGICAL REPORT, August, 1966, pp. 115-118.

10. Clinard, M., SOCIOLOGY OF DEVIANT BEHAVIOR (New York: Holt, 1963); Peters, E.L., "Public school attitudes toward juvenile delinquents," JOURNAL OF RESEARCH IN CRIME AND DELINQUENCY, 6:56-62, 1969.

11. Op. cit., supra note 8.

12. Op. cit., supra note 3.

13. Op. cit., supra note 8.

14. Berman, A., "Delinquents are disabled," in Kratoville, B. (ed.), YOUTH IN TROUBLE (San Rafael, Cal.: Academic Therapy, 1974).

15. Redl, F., Paper presented to 20th Annual Meeting, Mental Health Association of Southeastern Pennsylvania, November 11, 1971.

16. Roman, M., REACHING DELINQUENTS THROUGH READING (Springfield, Ill., 1957).

17. Swift, M. and Back, L., "A method for aiding teachers of the troubled adolescent," ADOLESCENCE, 8:1-16, 1973.

THE CHILDCARE APPRENTICESHIP PROGRAM: AN EXPERIMENT IN CROSS-AGE INTERVENTION

Hayden Duggan
John Shlien
Harvard University

The Childcare Apprenticeship Program was a three-year experiment at the Robert W. White Alternative School in Boston in which delinquent and disturbed adolescents worked with much younger children (1). Some of the younger children were from the same neighborhoods as the adolescents; others came from clinical daycare programs for autistic and schizophrenic children, and still others from community centers in the area. A primary goal of the project was to encourage prosocial behavior on the part of the adolescents described as acting-out or antisocial and generally considered too troubled to take on any significant amount of responsibility. The experiment sought to answer two fundamental questions: Can "bad" kids do good? And will it change them?

The conceptual base for this cross-age intervention effort was empathy — the responsiveness of one individual to another. The literature on empathy in children and young adolescents suggests a relationship between healthy personality development and the acquisition of empathic responses. Empathy entails concern for others, and the ability to correctly perceive the plight of another is viewed as a crucial element. If a person lacks the capacity to comprehend another's distress, then an empathic response can hardly be expected. Since it is possible that an individual could be sufficiently disturbed to be unaware of the emotional needs of another, a major question addressed by the experimental program was whether or not young delinquents possess the ability to empathize with others.

The emphasis on development of empathy in delinquent youth stemmed from the school's underlying assumption, originally formulated by Harvard psychologist Robert White, that the desire for competence is a motivating factor in all human behavior. The staff of the Robert W. White School is dedicated to finding and exploiting any sources of competence in its adolescent students, most of whom have had very limited opportunities to succeed in any area of their lives. The Childcare Apprenticeship Program, then, represented an effort to promote a specific sense of competence: development of empathy, compassion and the ability to care for others.

ANTECEDENTS OF THE CHILDCARE EXPERIMENT

The Childcare Apprenticeship Program grew out of the need to give disruptive students an opportunity to take responsibility and demonstrate competence as an alternative to acting-out or delinquent behavior. Students at the Robert W. White School had been having difficulty concentrating on classroom activities, especially in the afternoons, and they frequently engaged in violent or destructive acts both on and off school grounds. Students typically were alert and functional in the morning hours, but lunch period became a breeding ground for fights and by early afternoon staff had to struggle to maintain students' interest and prevent or control disruptive behavior. If no activities or field trips were planned, students often released tension by such acts as setting off fire extinguishers or vandalizing cars in adjacent parking lots.

One cause of such behavior is boredom, which grew out of lack of opportunities to experience feelings of competence and responsibility. One answer was to create a strong afternoon program which placed heavy demands on students for responsible behavior while offering them an opportunity to experience both competence and the feeling of being needed. The childcare program appeared to satisfy these requirements, but there was some resistance, among both school staff and the clinical services committee of the local mental health center, to the notion of using disturbed and delinquent adolescents to work with needy children. While there were many examples of successful cross-age therapeutic and pre-vocational programs in prisons, hospitals, and nursing homes, there was some apprehension about the use of this approach with this particular population.

Considerable planning and advance preparation thus was needed before the program could be launched. The experiment began with a one-year "pre-pilot" project in which the School donated space for classes for autistic children with the provision that several Robert White students would be hired as trainee childcare workers. In this phase of the program four adolescent workers were closely observed and the elements of the larger experimental program were developed.

THE "PRE-PILOT" PHASE

In the pre-pilot phase of the program, staff were interested in determining whether delinquent and disturbed adolescents could work successfully with young children and, if so, what characteristics were especially desirable in adolescent childcare workers. The program was interested only in those adolescents who, despite their disturbed or delinquent behavior, had basic affiliative potential and whose disturbance, though not temporary, was primarily reactive and situational. The problem, then, was how to identify those adolescents who, despite histories of serious clinical disturbance or delinquency involvement, might have the potential for working with others and how a mutually beneficial experience for both child and adolescent could be assured.

The pre-pilot experience did provide some indicators for use in selection of trainees. Successful childcare workers were enthusiastic about the work and showed a sincere interest in the children. They were able to appreciate individual differences and the needs of each child and they displayed great patience in their interactions with the children. Some of the adolescents — who, it must be remembered, had been referred to the Robert W. White School because they were unmanageable in the public school setting — were surprisingly successful in the childcare program. The experience of being able to reach and help children with problems — even those whom professional staff had not been able to reach — in some cases produced dramatic changes in these adolescents.

In general, it was found that obviously troubled youth could be excellent teacher aides, childcare assistants, and daycare trainees. They had to be supervised, reminded forcefully about the importance adults place on such things as schedules and showing up to work even on a beautiful day. They had to be encouraged and never taken for granted, for their interest in the work was directly related to the recognition they received as being trustworthy, and being wanted. Staff also found that the more was asked of the childcare workers, and the higher the standards expected of them, the more responsibly they acted. If they did not follow through they expected to be disciplined. Staff never had to "walk on eggshells" because of anyone's past problems.

Most important, none of the adolescents acted out in the presence of the children with whom they were working, no matter what they said or did to their counselors afterwards. This, of course, is the base line of all such cross-age experiments. And it is the unspoken fear that causes professionals to be cautious in becoming involved: what if these adolescents display their pathology to the point where the children are jeopardized? It is a reasonable fear and constitutes, in fact, the major dividing line between adolescents who can and cannot be childcare workers. As the program unfolded over the course of three years, childcare workers consistently avoided acting out in front of their young charges. This was, of course, in large part due to careful selection — the *sine qua non* of the entire approach.

SELECTION AND ORIENTATION

To other practitioners contemplating a cross-age approach with troubled adolescents, it must be stressed that there is no by-passing a substantial and careful selection process. The program is not for everyone and its selectivity must be clear from the outset. During the first actual "pilot" year, the restrictive selection procedure, which resembled "trying out for a team," actually raised the status of childcare in the eyes of street-hardened kids. There were two primary approaches to selection. One was an individual rating on a measure of empathy constructed by program staff for the purpose. Another was a "reality check" on both test results and the personal impressions of staff which consisted of a two-month orientation and trial period.

On most standard measures of intelligence or projective tests of personality or emotional state, populations such as that of the Robert White School show up in distorted and inaccurate numbers or profiles which neither capture their genuine strengths nor point out their weaknesses in ways helpful to program planning. The Measure of Empathy developed by staff for the Childcare Apprenticeship Program does reflect such strengths and weaknesses, primarily because it was created from the concerns of these adolescents as heard over four years of counseling. Although most useful when employed in conjunction with direct observation and experience with a particular youth, it proved to be a reliable predictor of program success.

The test is comprised of three tape-recorded stories, each followed by the same five questions. The first story represents the base line of empathic awareness: a child raises a puppy in the projects, nurturing its healthy growth, only to have it disappear one night due to the carelessness of an older sibling. The second story taps family issues of feeling unappreciated, wanting to contribute but never doing it "right," and lacking money. The third story, involving a grandfather and an adolescent, was difficult for the younger adolescents to grasp, just as the first one elicited fairly stock answers from the oldest ones. If a childcare trainee could not relate to any of the stories, the individual inevitably was not successful as a child-care worker. If a particular story drew a disproportionate reaction, personal knowledge of the adolescent was utilized to determine whether this was a result of over-identification with real-life events or an accurate measure of empathic potential.

The five questions were: (1) How do you think the character in the story feels? (2) Have you ever been in that situation? (3) If you were in the character's place, what would you do? (4) How does it make you feel to think about it? (5) If you were the character's friend, and you knew how he or she felt, what would you do? The first question is a test of basic cognitive accuracy: does the subject understand the problem? The second question tests for experience with the situation, while the third is an experience in role-playing (especially if the subject has not experienced a similar problem). The fourth question tests for degree of affective response (empathy), as does the fifth question in a more active way. The significance attached to these last two questions is symbolic of the program's whole approach to empathy and its value in working with troubled adolescents. Empathy is a pro-social quality implying concern for others no matter how harshly life may have treated oneself. Encouraging empathic responses, then, means removing the interpersonal barriers and anonymity which help to make antisocial acts easier.

The second phase of selection and orientation, the two-month trial period, was designed to test primarily for motivation, not acting-out behavior, since it was known that prior levels of acting out had little to do with childcare potential. What mattered was genuine interest in working with a child. Orientation consisted of three types of activity: group meetings, practice field trips, and role-playing. In group meetings staff discussed their own childhood impressions, the ways in which children differ from adolescents as adolescents differ from adults, and the kinds of needs that small children may express. In practice field trips childcare trainees visited local museums, zoos, puppet shows, and other children's activities in order to gain an appreciation of how such activities may differ when one is concerned with more than one's own needs. Students then presented oral or written reports on their field experiences to staff members and discussed the suitability of various trips for young children. Role-playing offered the adolescents a chance to express their knowledge of children's feelings and views of the world. Later, trainees also wrote practice letters to the parents of children with whom they might be paired.

Selection of 12 childcare finalists out of 19 serious applicants and 27 students involved in the orientation process was not really very difficult. Students whose reaction to the Empathy Measure was energetic and caring and who also were demonstrably trustworthy with a child were offered the available positions. Pay was the same as for all other student employment jobs at the school, $2.50 an hour, and students were scheduled for two hours each afternoon they worked (minimum twice weekly). They were given permission forms for their parents to sign, followed up by individual conferences with every parent and adolescent involved in the program. An Overview Committee served a watchdog function, with the power to close down the program and to monitor it unannounced.

The importance of this entire orientation period, which lasted roughly ten weeks, reached far into the program's future. Of the original 12 childcare workers, nine were still with the program two years later. The orientation had confirmed the belief that, despite sometimes cruel childhood experiences, many troubled adolescents were willing and able to give love and attention to young children in a responsible manner.

THE CHILDCARE PROGRAM

In the year-long pilot and the experimental program which followed, 34 Robert W. White School students worked with staff — some only briefly, others for as long as three years — to serve a total of 28 children in the School playroom or in other community daycare programs (2). Eight field settings were explored, and by the end of the program four of these were using Robert White student workers on a regular basis. Four childcare workers, all graduates of the School, subsequently became non-clinical staff members.

The immense value of non-traditional, paraprofessional modes of helping, provided good support and supervision are present, was clearly demonstrated. The program became a genuine cross-age experiment, with staff (other than clinicians) consisting of three older adolescent graduates of the Robert W. White School and a parent of a childcare worker. The crux of the experience remained the playroom interaction. The playroom was open from early afternoon until 5:30 or 6 p.m., and three adolescent-child pairs worked there each day. Clay, finger-painting, magic shows, gross-motor activities, reading readiness, tower-building with blocks, puzzles, toy trucks, collages, and cake parties gradually expanded until the entire back section of the School was cordoned off into two additional rooms. It was not unusual to see an autistic child, a multiply-handicapped and terminally ill young boy, and several children from the community playing in parallel and often cooperative fashion. Occasionally they were joined by staff members' children; always they were supervised by clinical staff and student coordinators. From the playroom, field trips and home visits were made regularly.

Placement of childcare workers in other community daycare centers was preceded by an observation period of at least two weeks in the school playroom. Adolescents who chose to move out into other settings generally differed somewhat from those who preferred the playroom, tending to show fewer clinical problems, a stronger sense of pre-vocational mission, and less need for a special one-to-one relationship with a child. The success of daycare placements was mixed, depending on the setting. The most important variable was whether or not the adolescent was genuinely needed: Childcare workers would travel across half the city to a setting in which they felt welcome and useful. They would not go five blocks if they felt merely tolerated and were used only for errands.

Pairing of adolescents and children was done with great care, with a typical trial period lasting six weeks. A good deal of encouragement usually was needed in the beginning, but if a pair were well launched, solid and lasting cross-age friendships were formed. For the adolescent paired with a child in his or her own community, often the gains in self-esteem and sense of competence were especially marked, at least partially deriving from

194

increased respect from family and friends. The program became a source of pride and identity for a number of difficult youths who had suffered deprived childhoods.

The experience perhaps comes most alive in the words of the childcare workers themselves, some of whom established strong rapport with children so different from themselves that the precondition of perceived similarity seemed a far-fetched notion. Yet upon reflection and with time, it could be seen that the mutually constructive relationships were the result not of random good fortune, but of deeper levels of perceiving common need. For example, Joan, who went on to become a salaried counselor at her daycare placement, had often been described as selfish, lazy, and unmotivated. Yet, given the chance, she went far beyond what was asked of her.

Interviewer: Why do you want to keep working with us?
Subject: Because I enjoy the work I'm doing and I'm doing just what I want to be doing.
I: What do you get out of it?
S: The pleasure of knowing that Kevin is enjoying himself...
I: Why did you specifically want to work with autistic children?
S: Because I'd worked with them before and they are fun to work with.
I: Why did you like working with them so much?
S: 'Cause they needed help.
I: And you feel that maybe you've got something special with those kids?
S: Yes. They're definitely different, and when I work with them I feel like my help is useful and they can use me and I can use them. I'm doing something. I'm not just sitting there and watching someone else play. I mean, I participate in helping them in some way.
I: In what ways do you think you help them and in what ways do you think they help you?
S: What do I get from it? Well, I get a good feeling. I get a feeling that it does something to help them. And what do they get? I think they get just a little bit of love, a

little bit of understanding, and a little care — especially when they're not at home.

Another student, referred to the Robert W. White School for fighting, swearing, refusing to obey teachers, and even occasionally assaulting them, explained her success in the childcare program as follows:

> S: I have got patience. A lot of patience. Because if you don't have patience then you aren't going to be able to do nothing. You're gonna quit a job like that. You just won't be able to handle it.

This girl, who worked in a clinical daycare setting with schizophrenic and autistic children, succeeded in establishing an emotional relationship with a child whom professionals had failed to reach. Her explanation was simple:

> I: Why do you think you were able to do this with her?
> S: Well, she felt a lot more relaxed, and I tried to be really nice to her and I explained to her — it's good for you...more on her own level, kind of my own, so she did understand what was being said and what it meant...

CONCLUSION

This experiment in cross-age intervention demonstrated the utility of such an approach in aiding the healthy development of adolescents who have not been helped by other strategies. The cross-age approach can be used to achieve therapeutic or pre-vocational benefits, and it can be adapted to a multitude of settings, populations, and supervisory resources. A very wide range of service delivery settings, from hospital waiting rooms to cooperative inner-city nursery schools could absorb adolescent enthusiasm and talents, provided the spontaneous nature of each commitment and the definite need for adult presence are respected. Each implementation, of course, will vary according to the type of service program and the characteristics of both sets of clients, the helpers and the helped.

It should be re-emphasized that selection criteria are crucial to this approach. Measures to assess warmth or coldness, outgoingness or shyness abound if one chooses to avoid traditional personality instruments. The measure of empathy used in this program, tailored specifically for its population, proved an effective predictor of potential childcare ability. Interestingly, with proper selection, orientation, and pairing, the more seriously disturbed adolescents proved to be the most dedicated and enthusiastic childcare workers. High "perceived similarity" between adolescent and child often was found to exist on more subtle and complex dimensions than color or neighborhood.

The value of the cross-age childcare program in reducing disruptive classroom behavior and delinquent acts on and around school grounds was found to be exceptional. Apparently, to the extent that school crime is reactive or situational, it can be prevented by offering demanding but meaningful programs to those who are capable of benefitting from such help. The advantage of an experience such as the Childcare Apprenticeship Program appears to lie in the actual demonstration of competence, the assumption of real responsibility, and the consensual validation of self-worth which comes not just from a counselor's encouragement, but from direct feedback given by the child, the supervisor and peers. It is important to be helped in therapy to accept and like oneself, but to be able to see and experience one's own competence, and to feel it reflected in the trust and affection of another, certainly is of equal if not greater value.

FOOTNOTES

1. Supported by funds from NIMH, Massachusetts Department of Public Welfare, Department of Special Education, Division of Youth Services, Boston School Committee, Mayor's Committee on Safe Streets

(LEAA), the School was developed under the auspices of the Harvard Graduate School of Education and operates in a wing of the Erich Lindemann Community Mental Health Center. Open Harbor, Inc., a non-profit corporation, oversees both the School and the Childcare Apprenticeship program.

2. Following the official pilot year of the program, funding was obtained from the Department of Health, Education and Welfare through the Boston office of Child Abuse and Neglect. A full description of the program is available from the authors. Also see: Duggan, H.A., ADOLESCENCE: A SECOND CHANCE, to be published by D. C. Heath, Lexington Books, 1978. The timetable of the program was: 1974-75 — Pre-Pilot Year (individual placements; no formal program); 1975-76 — Pilot Year (Childcare Apprenticeship Program created, funded by Robert White School), and 1976-77 — Experimental year, program funded by Office of Child Development (Abuse and Neglect).

TOMORROW'S EDUCATION:
MODELS FOR PARTICIPATION

Ernst Wenk
Responsible Action
Davis, California

Recent years have witnessed a fundamental political shift within our society. It appears to press toward more direct citizen participation in the democratic process — a development that could transform our basic political structure. Education emerges as a guiding force in this development and a redefinition of the varied roles of education in our society seems inevitable. Educational approaches to social problem-solving seem to have greater potential than some other models that have been tried. Legal and medical models, for example, have been proved inadequate in dealing with alcoholism, drug abuse, crime, and delinquency. Educational approaches do not prescribe solutions but rather provide a process through which solutions can be found or created. Ideally, the educational process draws its energies and its direction from the involvement of active participants. Such problem-solving approaches contain the ingredients needed for interactive (democratic) government, but they also foster individual growth and improved mental health. Education, in this model, is the central force for community development as well as a key to personal development and well-being.

We have neglected community participation in problem-solving. For too long we have looked outside our communities for solutions to social problems. Federal and state aid available for help in improving education, reforming criminal and juvenile justice, providing welfare and better health services, have led us to believe that the roots of our social problems and their solutions lie outside the community. It has become fashionable to rely on

199

distant, impersonal government bureaucracies, to see ourselves as neither part of the problem nor part of the solution. We appear to have forgotten that many social problems are rooted in families and local communities and that actions aimed at problem-solving must originate in the community and neighborhood if they are to have maximum impact.

No doubt there is a need for federal and state programs to bring about some equalization in the distribution of resources or to stimulate new and innovative programs which, after an initial period, can be supported from local sources. But if our communities are to be revitalized, and if we are to find better solutions to problems that manifest themselves in the community, the *initiative* for change must come from the communities themselves. Communities must design, implement, and maintain community-based problem-solving structures that are controlled by local residents and involve a reasonable cross-section of all those affected by their decisions and actions.

Unfortunately, most communities are ill-prepared for such an undertaking. The present paper presents two educational innovations that may be helpful in working toward the goal of interactive community development. Neither program has been designed specifically to prevent or control juvenile crime or other misbehavior in school and in the surrounding community. Both, however, could have considerable impact on juvenile delinquency and youth crime. Each is supported by a significant body of theoretical literature and practical experience indicating that its assumptions are sound and its methods generally effective in preventing delinquency and in interrupting what appears to be a causal chain leading from school failure to school crime. Some of the areas that are relevant in this regard are curriculum tracking, perceived lack of linkage between schools and communities, perceived irrelevance of the schooling process by many students, low student commitment to school, lack of involvement by students in educational planning and decision-making, and lack of many peer teaching opportunities for students.

Partnership in Research, tested in New Hampshire and further developed following initial evaluation, is essentially a youth involvement strategy. It also has roots in one branch of social action theory, particularly in that reflected by what Donald T. Campbell has called the "experimental society" — a society in which progress is made by integrating the best of science and democracy (1). The Integrated Community Education System is basically a community involvement strategy. It envisions a radical restructuring of the educational system to provide for flexible and largely self-initiated programming for people of all ages and an open-ended school system which allows for life-long experiential learning.

PARTNERSHIP IN RESEARCH

The Partnership in Research strategy assumes that knowledge acquired through active learning has a more significant impact than learning by passive acceptance. The transitory nature of knowledge also is imparted by this approach: knowledge gained through activity is experienced as a time-bound, situation-bound phenomenon requiring constant updating to be continually relevant. Partnership in Research is designed to keep the individual sensitive to an inquiry type of knowledge that encourages self-discovery, adaptation, and personal development — a basic mental posture that it is hoped will be adopted as a life-long strategy of learning and growth.

The PIR strategy was tested in spring 1972 in a New Hampshire senior high school (2). The prime interest was to involve as many students as possible in defining some of their major concerns with respect to the school setting. It was hoped that increased understanding of the educational setting might lead students to learn about school-related factors that contribute to social problems, such as juvenile delinquency and youth crime, school non-involvement, and dropping out. The high school, situated in a medium-large New England city, had a student population of close to 2,000 students in grades 9 through 12. Like most schools in the United States, it was co-educational.

During meetings between the vice-principals and research staff, a decision was made to initiate the project during the school's English periods. This ensured that practically all students would be reached initially. English classes remained the major source of communication between the project and the students, but the actual work of the project was an extracurricular option for the students.

PHASE 1: PLANNING AND INITIATION

Project staff made preliminary contacts with some students and teachers and prepared a questionnaire asking students to name three of the most pressing concerns or problems they felt needed attention in the school. The questionnaires were presented and the study explained to each English class by project staff, starting with the senior classes and recruiting and instructing volunteer senior students, who then acted as assistants, administering questionnaires and introducing the study to the junior, sophomore, and freshman classes. This completed the first step in turning the study over to the students.

Besides the initial questionnaire, each student in grades 9 through 12 received a questionnaire to give to his parents. Parent questionnaires asked about priorities of concerns and whether or not parents should be involved in this kind of study. Teachers received a similar questionnaire, as did the janitorial staff and the food services staff. Also, each student who had dropped out during the current school year received a questionnaire and was asked to designate a student still in school who would act as a liaison between himself and the study.

PHASE 2: FORMING STUDENT TASK FORCES

The return rate of the questionnaires filled out by the students was close to 100 percent. One-third of the teaching staff and approximately 5 percent of the parents returned the questionnaires. There were practically no responses from the janitorial and food services staff or from students who had dropped out earlier in the school year (which may suggest a feeling of isolation predominant in these groups).

Eight major topics surfaced that led to the formation of student task forces or study groups to look into the following student concerns:

1. *School Rules.* This group was to study school regulations and measures taken at the school, as well as the relationship between school, police, and the courts.

2. *Race Relations.* This group was to study ways to improve race relations among students. Concerns were particularly expressed by students who experienced during the previous school year serious disruptions in school because of racial conflicts.

3. *Drug Misuse.* This study group was interested in looking into student involvement in drug misuse and presenting some suggestions for coping with this problem.

4. *School Programs for the Non-College-Bound Student.* This study group was to investigate programs available to the student seeking a vocational career and needing preparation to enter the labor market.

5. *School Programs for the Academically Inclined Student.* This study group was to look at programs for the college-bound student.

6. *Student Roles.* This group was to study the roles of the high-school student, his rights and responsibilities. They were to focus on the way students can be involved in curriculum planning and other aspects of the administration of the school. This group's emphasis was central to the major study objective of mobilizing untapped student resources.

7. *School and Community.* This group was to study the

relationships of the school to the community, the voters, the taxpayers, and the authorities (such as the School Board), and to come up with suggestions to improve these relationships.

8. *The Drop-out Problem.* This study group was to interview school drop-outs and planned to develop alternative educational programs for students who feel alienated from most current educational programs.

All groups began with a nucleus of a few students who were highly involved in the particular issue and who volunteered to recruit additional students to help with various study tasks. Special efforts were made to keep established student leaders from taking over the study group by assigning traditionally active students, already in leadership roles in the school, to individual assignments in the project that were independent of the study groups. Leadership positions in the study groups thus were open to students who previously had little opportunity to express themselves or take leadership. This gave the project the opportunity to mobilize untapped student resources while still making use of active student leaders for important tasks outside the study groups.

PHASE 3: STUDY GROUP PROJECTS

During Phases 3 and 4, a recently graduated college student, who had experience in working with groups, was the resident project staff at the school. She acted as advisor and liaison among the project, the teaching staff, and the school administration. While the initiative was left primarily to students, coordination and assistance were actively provided by giving support as soon as the need was perceived.

With the help of the director of the business department, the research assistant set up an office space for the project. Two students from the business department were employed part-time by the project under a student work program. This project

204

office provided services to the various study groups and maintained contact with the students.

The various study groups of volunteer students went about their business in their own ways. One group decided to interview local citizens about their attitudes toward smoking, alcohol, drugs, open campus, or school rules. Another group interviewed dropouts. One group, after several meetings and uncomfortable discussions, got scared and disbanded, but not before they had designed and administered a questionnaire probing racial attitudes. The group studying academic programs designed a questionnaire and administered some, but the group lost interest generally.

Two groups were quite active and involved, and carried out productive programs. The vocational program group presented plans for students, in conjunction with staff, to run the cafeteria on a business-like basis in order to learn the food services trade. They also proposed to develop and operate a school-based communications center with its own 5-mile radius radio station, video studio for intramural T.V., and a student newspaper. They made a field trip to a neighboring state to visit a student-operated radio station and reported back to the project.

The drug abuse group probably was the most active and most involved. Each student had a good reason to be part of this group. One was a former heroin user who returned to school after treatment to finish his requirements for a high-school diploma. Others had had experiences with drugs or had brothers, sisters, or friends who used drugs, or parents with an alcohol problem. Some were just deeply concerned about what they saw happening around them. This group visited local facilities for drug prevention and treatment, designed and administered a questionnaire, compiled some of the results, and conducted a workshop at the end of the project.

PHASE 4: WORKSHOPS

Four groups conducted workshops during the last week of

the project. These included the groups studying drug use, school rules, vocational curriculum, and student roles. The panels were composed of students, while other students and teachers were the participating audience. These meetings were videotaped and replayed for students at the school to pass on some of the information and ideas generated by these activities.

SUMMARY RESULTS

This peer-conducted research effort demonstrated that high-school students, working under their own volition, can develop questions and identify issues that are highly relevant to their own interests and development. The collection of data actually was secondary to the real goal of this endeavor, which was to involve students in observing and evaluating issues that have a significant impact on their lives.

The project was exploratory and had only limited financial backing. These restrictions were offset by the enthusiastic support the study received from students and from some of the school staff. It is recommended that future attempts to carry out PARTNERSHIP IN RESEARCH projects be made part of the regular school curriculum, rather than appended to the school program as an extracurricular activity. This kind of scientific inquiry then could develop a tradition of its own and become, for certain research projects, more sophisticated in research methodology. Projects then might focus on other problems, not directly related to the school, that are of special interest to students.

The findings of the study groups were modest and the methods employed were relatively unsophisticated. Yet, the method and the findings are valuable from several points of view:

1. Interesting facts were uncovered.

2. The project gave students the opportunity to make a deep, personal commitment to an activity that was

aimed, in part, at learning more successful coping strategies.

3. The project provided an example of a democratic educational experience by giving students the opportunity to act as independent participants and by showing respect for their critical insights.

4. The sharing of decision-making gave the students the opportunity to experience an existential equality with the adults involved.

5. The open, honest, and objective confrontation with social problem issues provided a learning experience that seemed to enhance personal growth.

6. The learning that resulted from participation in the process of research seemed to produce a much deeper understanding than could be expected from the reading of a final report and listening to a lecture. The existential approach seems to facilitate acquisition of the learning and adaptive skills necessary for survival. The focus of this method on self-evaluation, self-help, self-development, self-growth, within both the individual and the group, should lead to continuing growth.

For many kinds of behavior, such as drug abuse, alcohol abuse, juvenile delinquency and youth crime in school and the community, legislation appears to be highly ineffective as a control mechanism. In fact, some laws and the difficulties inherent in their enforcement may simply aggravate the problem. Educational methods, such as PARTNERSHIP IN RESEARCH, may offer a more effective means of prevention and intervention. The study in New Hampshire was intended to provide exploratory material in support of this thesis.

THE INTEGRATED COMMUNITY EDUCATION SYSTEM

Partnership in Research might be particularly effective if it were part of an Integrated Community Education System (ICES) (3, 4). To the general public research is not an ally. The average citizen often perceives research as a tool of government or under the control of large corporate interests that tend to exploit the consumer. Until very recently, research has been preoccupied with peculiarities and deficiencies of individuals and little attention has been paid to deficiencies and injustices in government-provided services or to corporate actions that are in conflict with public interest. Specifically, social science has focused on individual "deviants" and their characteristics, almost totally neglecting environmental and social factors and their impact on individual behavior.

All this is changing. Science is beginning to serve more directly the public interest and may become a powerful tool for communal problem-solving. Donald T. Campbell proposes to create an "experimenting society" that makes science its servant and takes as its values the best of those of both democracy and science: honesty, open criticism, and a willingness to change in the face of new evidence. He calls for actions that integrate science and social concerns by adopting rigorous, rational, and scientific evaluations of new programs and ideas that allow further development of the best and modification or discontinuation of those that prove ineffective. Campbell suggests that we develop such evaluation research into a "folk science" that can be applied in a do-it-yourself fashion with voting-booth consequences.

The Integrated Community Education System (ICES) seems to hold promise for the creation of an informed and involved citizenry that can deal constructively with both the scientific aspects of social program development and the political constraints and consequences associated with responsible program decisions. The ICES is distinguished from other educational models in that it incorporates all of the following major features:

1. The system is planned, administered, and controlled by the community. ICES is created through intensive

community participation and responds in part to changing community needs.

2. ICES is based on the concept of life-long learning for all interested persons.

3. Most learning environments are multi-age.

4. Educational opportunities are flexible to meet individual objectives of students.

5. Two substantially different structures are the basis for all instruction:

   a. The General Education Structure operates learning environments that emphasize success and personal development while exploring subjects in a non-threatening way to broaden one's knowledge without the possibility of failure; and

   b. Career Education Structure operates learning environments which demand strict, disciplined learning that allows for serious and hard work toward skill development in the particular subject area.

6. Because of the multi-age learning environments and involvement of the community in their planning, administration, and control, ICES programs are envisioned as year-round educational programs.

The Integrated Community Education System has no narrowly defined educational programs or schools such as junior high, senior high, adult education, community college, or extension programs. Instead, a conceptually-based mode of instruction is offered for each of three different groups or levels:

Level I: Children, from birth to seven years of age

Level II: Children and youth, eight to fourteen years of age

Level III: Young adults and adults, fifteen years of age and older.

LEVEL I PROGRAMS

For children from birth to seven the mode consists of services directed toward need fulfillment and motivational, social, psychological, and physical development. This level, Comprehensive Children's Services, utilizes extensively students of all ages enrolled in level II and III programs, applying cross-age tutoring to its fullest with all the benefits that accrue for the student volunteer. At this level, services also are provided to parents directly. All level I programs are voluntary.

LEVEL II PROGRAMS

For children from eight to fourteen years, educational strategies are directed toward the further development of social and communicative skills as well as instruction in basic subjects. For this age group attendance is mandatory and students and teachers are held accountable for meeting certain educational standards.

LEVEL III PROGRAMS

For the young adult and adult group, participation is again voluntary and the individual selects his own educational objectives with the help of an educational guidance counselor. The educational opportunities available at this level, including personal development as well as academic, vocational, and social skill development, permit any number of combinations of these different programs at any one time. Education for the young adult and adult consists of a life-long process of learning and teaching, since teaching or tutoring others at any of the three levels becomes a part of the individual's own learning and growth.

MAJOR ICES PROGRAM FEATURES:
COMPREHENSIVE CHILDREN'S SERVICES

Noting the results of recent educational, psychological, and medical research documenting the crucial importance of the first eight years of life (5), Wilson Riles, Superintendent of Instruction for the State of California, sought and received benchmark legislation that allows for the development of comprehensive plans for early childhood education. Early childhood education is one of the principal components of the Integrated Community Education System, but the latter goes beyond the early childhood education concept to include Comprehensive Children's Services for the youngest target group — children from birth to seven years of age. These services would be provided on a community basis through neighborhood children's centers operated by professional child care staff who receive maximum support (professional services and student participation on a voluntary and paid basis) from other components of the Integrated Community Education System.

Neighborhood children centers would be numerous, well equipped, and prepared for quality service to children and their parents. Parents could bring their small children any time to the neighborhood children's center where professional services would be available. The emphasis would be on making them content while they are there, to provide them with comfortable shelter and food, to play with them, and to give them attention and love regardless of their background or home environment. All these services would be provided by students from the Integrated Community Education System, working under the supervision and guidance of professional staff.

Everyone involved would benefit from such a system of children's centers. The children would experience warmth and comfort and over the years would develop a strong positive attitude toward the community. Parents would utilize these centers as a welcome resource. They would be offered opportunities to take part in in-service education to learn child-rearing and child care, thus enabling them to become more effective parents. Student employees or volunteers would derive great satisfaction from the services they provided and would themselves learn a great deal from their participation in in-service education in child care and development. The community would benefit from the early identification and fulfillment of the needs of children and youth.

In our preoccupation with machines, we have come to expect a gas station on almost every street corner. If service stations are not abundantly available to take care of our cars, we feel that vital resources are missing. It is time that we perceived the critical lack of resources to serve children and young people and to insist that these resources be provided and developed.

ICES PROGRAM STRUCTURES: GENERAL AND CAREER EDUCATION

Under the ICES model, the student aged seven or older has the option to choose programs in two basic education structures: general education or career education. Students who successfully complete certain career education requirements have the further option of entering higher education through the professional education structure, which is equivalent to our present college-level instruction. The term "career education" as used in this paper should not be confused with vocational training or trade training. As used here, the term refers to any disciplined learning that has clearly defined objectives. These basic structures, with their differing educational objectives and methods, provide the depth and diversity that give the individual the freedom to construct his own educational program to fit his particular needs. The teacher also is provided with a variety of teaching environments, enabling him to express his own teaching style and pursue his own interests.

The core of both the general education structure and the career education structure is the classroom or a class module. As the educational pioneer Pestalozzi put it, "a country's future is decided in its classrooms." It is equally true that the individual's future is decided in the classroom. In our culture, the classroom is − potentially, at least − the most universally available environment for learning, thinking, and exchanging ideas, for maintaining perspective, for practicing equality and justice, and for encouraging respect and love for others. The classroom should be a "laboratory of life" in both a personal and a communal sense.

GENERAL EDUCATION

General education provides for learning activities designed primarily to enrich and to motivate without fear of failure. Activities are exploratory, and structured to encourage the student to seek out, for as many subjects as he wishes, the more demanding educational programs offered in career education. It should be possible to fulfill minimum educational requirements by attending general education classes and achieving a level of reading, writing, and arithmetic that fulfills the requirements set by the state. Most individuals probably would combine general education classes with career education classes; the teacher of general education classes would place primary emphasis on the general welfare of the student as an individual. In addition to presenting subject matter in a nonthreatening and collaborative manner, the teacher in this educational environment would pay a great deal of attention to the personal needs of his students. The subject matter or class focus becomes a means of achieving multi-faceted goals related to personal development and individual growth.

A concrete example of how these general education classes are envisioned is shown in the foreign language module, such as French. In general education, individuals of varied backgrounds meet for an introduction to the French language and culture. A variety of aspects related to the French culture such as music, philosophy, politics, cooking, and sports are explored. Exposure to the language would be provided through records, tapes, films, and conversation. No specific learning objectives would be set because the education structure of general education is motivational and enrichment-oriented rather than achievement-oriented to meet preconceived objectives.

Naturally, this multi-age, multi-background student group may learn a limited amount of French that would be useful in travel abroad or in future professional work. However, students could expect to have a pleasurable educational experience that widens their horizons. For some, the program may prepare them for a more demanding program in French under the career education structure. Similar exploratory treatments of other subjects, such as science, mathematics, history, homemaking, or vocational skills, would be presented in learning environments conducted by competent teachers who are primarily motivators and facilitators of growth for their students.

Another example of a general education class module is the physical education program. Within the general education structure traditional team-based competition would be discouraged. Exercises and sports would be undertaken for enjoyment. Individuals of all skill levels would be accommodated, and teams necessary for certain games would be frequently reconstituted to provide variety in team composition and to foster non-specific competition.

There is much to be learned from the non-competitive educational structure in which, while the individual is not graded, the class as a whole may develop its own "grading" system to address questions of the benefits and relevance of the learning activities on a class-wide basis. They may consider the contribution not only of the teacher but of the students as well.

CAREER EDUCATION

The learning environment within the career education structure is substantially different from that of the general education structure. Career education classes have specific learning objectives that will be met throughout the class sessions. Students of different backgrounds and ages are grouped together by virtue of their common educational objectives. Participating students voluntarily subscribe to disciplined and specifically goal-oriented activities that can be carried out only if efforts by the students and the teachers toward reaching class goals are consistently maintained. The pay-off for these efforts are the skills learned as specified in the class objectives. Therefore, students and teachers are highly motivated to achieve in the particular subject chosen. Career education courses lead to higher education or professional education as higher education is an extension of the strict, disciplined career education structure.

In contrast to the French class in the general education structure, a career French class is clearly devoted to teaching specific language skills. For example, French I has a clearly defined beginning and a clearly defined end. French II builds on French I with its own clearly defined objectives. The career education structure with its career credit system allows a person to pursue particular skills throughout the career structure and beyond by moving into the professional education structure that is represented by our university and higher education system. The professional education structure, for example, would provide an individual with qualifications as a French teacher or certified interpreter.

In physical education, career education would include the highly competitive team membership or individual athletic achievement that in today's schools, where few general education opportunities exist, excludes unfortunately many students from sports activities.

Vocational training provides another example for contrasting the two basic education structures. In auto mechanics the general education structure would offer programs that expose the students in a disciplined way (no education can proceed without discipline with respect to the educational environment and the maintenance of equipment and tools) to auto mechanics. These courses would be motivational and exploratory, but might also include arrangements for the student to get work experience in an operating auto mechanics business in the community. Then, when the individual is ready to accept the challenge of career training, and is willing to expend the effort to acquire professional auto mechanic skills, he must either enroll in a career education class with specific educational objectives in this field, or he must enter into a formal apprenticeship agreement with an operating business in the community.

These two educational structures complement each other. They replace tracking students by allowing the student to tailor his education to his own needs through a combination of components from both educational structures. The opportunity for the individual to participate in the design of his own educational plan (including any combination of exploratory general classes and strict career classes) and the opportunity to keep educational options open throughout life are the main features of the Integrated Community Education System.

Many of the alternatives available in traditional schools appear limiting and often degrading. Continuation high school, low-achiever tracks, and special programs for the educationally handicapped provide little variety or flexibility. An appropriate combination of general education and career education would allow a person to escape labeling or identification as a member of a low-status program. Most slow learners are not slow in all subjects. This approach gives the youth who needs primarily general education classes the opportunity to explore in greater depth an area in which he feels the greatest motivation and competence. He may enroll in the career class in auto mechanics or physical education, for instance, while remaining in the general education structure for other subjects.

EDUCATIONAL REFORM AND DELINQUENCY PREVENTION

Both Partnership in Research and the Integrated Community Education System concept are directed toward the broader goals of revitalization of the community and its educational institutions. There are, however, some important implications for the prevention of youth crime and misbehavior which arise indirectly from such factors as: involvement of youth in their communities and in their own education; reduction of the artificial barriers which isolate young people from persons of both younger and older age groups; elimination of low-status educational groups (tracking, continuation schools, underachiever programs, etc.); involvement of youth and community residents in studying such problems as student crime and in designing solutions based on their own observations; increasing the importance of the student role within the school; improving the fit between the student and the learning environment; and reducing the split between student and teacher roles, and between the functions of teaching and learning, by combining each individual's own education with the tutoring of others.

If the strategy is to be set within a typology of "prevention" approaches, it can be viewed as *educational*, as opposed to the more common medical and legal models. In contrast to medical and legal approaches, the educational strategy assumes a basic outlook of growth and development and perceives the individual to be helped as student or "learner," a role that is maintained throughout life by many educated persons. The requirement of the medical approach that the person to be helped adopt the role of "patient" and the requirement of the legal approach that the person adopt the role of "criminal" or "delinquent" are viewed as detrimental to individual growth and maturation. These two requirements, and the stances generally adopted by mental health, criminal justice, and law enforcement professionals, tend to have stigmatizing effects and often are counterproductive by preventing social readjustment. The educational strategy does not need to apply negative labels (although frequently it, too, falls into this trap), but instead applies the supportive label of "student" that can enhance self-esteem and facilitate growth.

It is suggested that these and other learning models can be successfully applied in social problem-solving, particularly before sanctions based on medical models and legal models are employed. Such an approach may prevent a great many individuals from becoming "patients" or "convicts" by keeping them in a learning role as involved and motivated students. Education, then, might largely replace treatment, therapy, and correction, which could be reserved for less responsive persons and persons who present a serious danger to themselves and to others.

Partnership in Research, which involves public school students in the scientific examination of issues important to them, and the Integrated Community Education System, which anchors the public school to the local community, offer a unique opportunity to build a strong foundation for the experimenting society required for responsible change and problem-solving.

By bringing young people and other community residents into the process of experimental problem-solving, we can benefit from the utilization of as yet untapped human resources in our efforts to control delinquency and crime, alcoholism, drug addiction, and other social problems. By providing citizens with a means of effecting change through active participation in the democratic processes of government, we also can offer a viable alternative to apathy and irresponsible behavior. At the same time, we can move in the direction of an experimental society with local responsibility for and interest in the quality of its social programs and their rigorous evaluation.

FOOTNOTES

1. Tavris, Interview with Donald T. Campbell, PSYCHOLOGY TODAY, 1975.

2. This research was supported in part by a grant from the New Hampshire Governor's Commission on Crime and Delinquency to the Research Center of the National

Council on Crime and Delinquency and by General Research Support Grant 1SOL RR-05693-02 from the U.S. Public Health Service; Wenk, E., PEER CONDUCTED RESEARCH: A NOVEL APPROACH TO DRUG EDUCATION. Paper presented to the First International Congress on Drug Education, held at Montreux Vd., Switzerland, October 14-18, 1973.

3. Wenk, Ernst, "Schools and the community: A model for participatory problem-solving," in Wenk, E., (ed.), DELIN-QUENCY PREVENTION AND THE SCHOOLS: EMERG-ING PERSPECTIVES, CONTEMPORARY SOCIAL IS-SUES, Vol. 29, (Beverly Hills, CA: Sage Publications, 1976).

4. Wenk, Ernst, "Juvenile justice and the public schools: Mutual benefit through educational reform," JUVENILE JUSTICE, 1975, *26*, 7-14.

5. California State Department of Education, EARLY CHILDHOOD EDUCATION: REPORT OF THE TASK FORCE ON EARLY CHILDHOOD EDUCATION (Sacramento: Department of Education, 1972).

DEMOCRATIC EDUCATION AND THE PREVENTION OF DELINQUENCY

Peter Scharf
University of California at Irvine

In every major American urban area there is a school or group of schools that serves a special type of student. In New York City they are called the "600" schools. In California they are referred to as "continuation" schools. Elsewhere they are named "annexes," "discipline academies," or "special service schools." Whatever the label, the reality is obvious. This is the school for the child who has failed in the traditional school system. This school has a police cruiser parked near the gate. Many of its students have attacked at least one of the teachers. Here students get "released time" to meet with their probation officers. This is the school that everyone wishes were in some other part of town. This is *the* school.

Teachers in schools serving delinquent youth face careers filled with desperation and feelings of failure. I taught in such a school in an Eastern city, roughly ten years ago. During the course of a ten-month school year, no fewer than 12 of my 15 students left school. Tom Johnson was killed in a shoot-out with police. Five young women became pregnant. Two students, charged with being chronic runaways, were sent to a "junior republic." Three were convicted of felonies. One young man just left town.

Even more debilitating than the high casualty rate is the sense that what the teacher is required to do has no meaning for the students he faces every day. The textbooks have too many white faces. The discipline techniques demanded by the school board are intended for nervous suburban students. The tests devised by the city, the state, and school district become exercises in forced degradation. The administration seems more concerned with "covering up" atrocities committed upon and by students than with remedying the situation. Materials given the teacher either are impossible for these students to read or bear no relationship to students' lives. At professional meetings, other teachers talk about cognitive development, learning objectives, and teacher accountability. No one wants to talk about how to keep Jack from jumping out the window or a tactful way to tell Sam not to smoke pot in the back row. No one knows what to tell the teacher to do when Alan (who has already assaulted a dozen people) looks at you with those angry eyes.

THE NEED FOR THEORY

Goals appropriate to the education of delinquent youth must have philosophical, psychological, and sociological roots. They must posit clear ends to direct the educational effort, offer learning principles appropriate to youth with special problems, and consider the socio-political perspective of the delinquent. Such goals rarely are articulated in a practical, yet intellectually supportable theoretical framework.

Delinquency theories are rife with intellectually counter-productive dichotomies. One such dichotomy centers on the simplistic notion that there are theories of the etiology of individual delinquency which stand in opposition to theories of group or collective delinquency. The theories of psychologists such as Erikson, Friedlander, and Skinner are posed in opposition to explanatory models which focus on either the dynamics of the delinquent subculture, e.g. by Cohen, Yablonski, Sutherland, and Matza, or on broader sociocultural dynamics, e.g. by Parks and Burgess, Miller, Merton, and Cloward and Ohlin (1 - 11).

The past twenty years also have witnessed a progressive separation between theories of cause and theories of action. Due in part to the desire of criminologists to dissociate them-

221

selves from action-oriented professions (such as social work and corrections), there has been an unhappy divorce of criminological theory, which attempts to explain delinquency as a social fact, from theories which are useful to professionals in working with individual delinquents. While there have been some exceptions to this trend (12), the concepts used by theoreticians more often are different from those adopted by action professionals.

Further, there is a widening gap between normative and empirical views of delinquency. In an apparent desire for respectability, mainstream criminologists often have presented their theories in the scientific language of cause and explanation, failing to see or masking the normative implications of their views. Moralists, on the other hand, often are blindly ideological, as exemplified by some of the "radical" criminologists who offer a clear moral position, but little scientific evidence for their assumptions.

Finally, there have been few efforts to develop interactive models of delinquency. Theories tend to stand in stark contrast to one another, forcing a choice between differential association and anomie theory or between behavioral and psychodynamic positions. Seldom have efforts been made to integrate varying criminological theories into more complex models.

An alternative to conventional approaches with delinquents is offered by the work of a group of researchers at Harvard University and the University of California who have sought to apply developmental psychologist, sociological, and ethical theories to the problem of delinquency. During the past eight years, this group has posited an educational approach using developmental psychology, testing it with student populations ranging from "normal" school children of different ages to sometimes disturbed and dangerous prisoners.

The methods used differ from traditional approaches in offering a theory of development which looks at the evolution of thinking in a social context. The theory offers discrete empirical and philosophical justifications for its assumptions and uses language suited to action as well as research. The perspective assumes that sociological, psychotherapeutic, and behavioral orientations to delinquency have ignored two critical dimensions. First, treatment and prevention programs rarely have focused upon the moral and legal reasoning of the delinquent; and second, there have been few effective efforts to create school environments which offer the potential delinquent a meaningful alternative social community.

To exemplify this perspective, we will begin by outlining the developmental perspective toward social reasoning, illustrating its educational importance with a description of a program for delinquent youths in a medium security prison in Connecticut. We will then turn to an effort to create a "democratic community" in a women's prison in Connecticut. Finally, we will attempt to show the importance of these programs for the education of youth who have had serious confrontations with the law.

A COGNITIVE-DEVELOPMENT APPROACH TO THE RE-EDUCATION OF DELINQUENTS

Research by Lawrence Kohlberg, conducted over a 25-year period, suggests that ideas about society progress through a sequence of six invariant stages. Each stage is considered a more adequate and comprehensive mode of thinking than less mature stages. Research findings indicate that the order of social development is the same in all societies, although the rate and ultimate stage reached may differ from one culture to the rest (13).

At Stage 1, there is an orientation toward punishment and obedience. Law is conceived as the force of the powerful to which the weaker submit. At Stage 2, "right" action becomes that which satisfies one's needs. Law is conceived in terms of expedience or a naive hedonism ("In America, the law says everyone can get what he wants"). Stage 3 offers what might be called the "good boy/girl" orientation. Law is associated with collective opinion: one obeys the law because that is what others expect. At Stage 4, there is a shift toward fixed definitions

223

of law and society. The law is justified in terms of its order-maintaining function ("Without law, the entire fabric of society would crumble"). Stage 5 is a legalistic-contract orientation. Law is a mutual contract among social equals, with the duties of the individual clearly defined and regulated. At Stage 6, Kohlberg argues, there is a rational basis for ethical decision-making. Here, the law is a repository of broader social principles and, where law and justice conflict, is subordinate.

The rate and extent of individual development are linked closely to the institutions with which one comes in contact. Broadly speaking, social institutions which encourage social role-taking and democratic dialogue are associated with rapid and more complete moral and social development. Institutions which are perceived by participants as just and equitable tend to stimulate mature moral thinking.

MORAL REASONING AND DELINQUENCY

A recent study by Kohlberg and Freundlich compared nonincarcerated delinquents of different ages with matched controls from similar social environments (14). Results from six samples revealed that delinquents tend to be markedly less mature than the controls. For example, while only 16 percent of the delinquents were reasoning at conventional levels, over 70 percent of the controls had attained at least a Stage 3 level of moral thinking. These observations imply that delinquents tend to be less morally mature than peers from similar environments. This does not mean that being lower staged causes delinquency, but it does suggest that most delinquents are recruited among less morally mature youth. It also suggests that one of the consequences of the delinquent label may be that a youth will remain in environments (e.g., prisons, foster care) that are not conducive to moral stage growth.

A few examples from a study of the moral ideologies of young offenders may illustrate some of the characteristics of delinquent thinking on moral issues. Each of the subjects in the study was presented with a series of dilemmas, including one which asks if it is right for a husband to steal a drug to save his dying wife. A Stage 1 male delinquent responded to this question as follows:

> No, he shouldn't. That's stealing. I wouldn't do no time for nobody, no matter what. I don't care if it was my wife. It doesn't matter . . . He will get bagged if he does that.

This subject's reasoning fails to differentiate even rational interests from a fear of punishment. Unfortunately, being afraid of punishment only rarely deters crime. This youth, for example, was arrested more than a dozen times during the next five years.

An example of Stage 2 reasoning provides what may be a typical offender response to the dilemma:

> Question: Should he steal the drug?
>
> Answer: Yah. Because if my wife was dying I'd want to save her. She's with me. I would want to keep her around. I would care for her.
>
> Question: What if she was sneaking around? They were about to get divorced.
>
> Answer: I'd say "later for her." You know what I mean? Why would he want her around then. I wouldn't be sticking my neck out for her.

This subject's Stage 2 hedonism is replaced by a morality of concern at Stage 3. Here the criteria of "rightness" becomes a matter of mutual expectations rather than simply a calculation of self-interest:

> Question: Should he have done that?
>
> Answer: Yes, I think he should have done it because his wife was dying and he needed the drug, and if there was some sort of law, or some

way he could have got the money besides him and his friend couldn't raise the money, so I feel that he did the right thing that he had left to do. A good husband wouldn't let his wife die.

While roughly half this sample of 16- to 20-year-old delinquents manifested some Stage 3 thinking, a far smaller proportion had developed what might be seen as substantial Stage 4 thinking. One exception was found in an interview with a 19-year-old "safe-cracker" who somehow emerged from a two-year prison sentence with a recognizably Stage 4 moral ideology:

Question: Do you think that Heinz should have done that? Was that wrong or right to break in?

Answer: I think Heinz was wrong even though he was in a peculiar situation where it was actually a matter of life and death. He was still stealing from a man who had developed this thing and it was his right to keep it because it was his possession. Heinz violated the man's rights by taking it. It's cut and dried . . . it was wrong to take this drug.

As rare as are Stage 4 thinkers among delinquents, even more rare is Stage 5 moral thought. One Stage 5 ex-offender was recently released from a California prison; he had been arrested for a politically motivated act of sabotage. In response to the Heinz dilemma, this man suggested:

It's not a question of the law. It's a matter of rightness. Like in my thing. I looked at the property laws of the state and said, hey, there's a more important issue here: *The War*. The same thing with this man. It's his wife's life versus the property of the state. He has an obligation to save her life.

While principled thinking is statistically rare among offenders, the most clearly moral individuals of any era are at risk of running afoul of the law. Jesus, Gandhi, and Socrates are but three moral philosophers who were imprisoned for transcending the law.

A PRISON INTERVENTION

The first efforts to apply this theory in an educational setting involved a series of moral discussion classes conducted by Kohlberg and Mosher (15), Blatt (16), Fenton (17), and their associates. These classes, conducted with groups of 15 to 20 students, attempted to pose prefabricated moral dilemmas involving issues such as the limits of confidentiality, euthanasia, or capital punishment. The goal of the discussions was to stimulate an increase in the maturity of student moral thinking. While these discussion groups proved effective in promoting students' moral development, it soon became evident that an effective program for delinquent youths required quite different dilemmas and techniques. To pilot these teaching strategies, the authors developed and implemented an experimental curriculum for delinquent youth in an Eastern medium-security prison.

The program was instituted by randomly establishing a 20-inmate experimental group. This group was divided into two discussion sections of ten inmates each who met separately for 36 (three sessions per week) two-hour sessions. In addition, a control group of 20 inmates was selected. All sessions were taped and transcribed. Of major concern at the outset of the study was whether a group of delinquents would be willing to discuss "abstract" moral dilemmas. The inmates, however, almost to a man, immediately became heatedly involved. There were few cases of unexplained absences and few silent pauses during the meetings.

As the program progressed, there was a gradual movement away from hypothetical dilemmas and toward the use of real-life dilemmas suggested by group members. One inmate, for example, suggested that the group discuss a dilemma about another inmate seeking prison favors by "ratting out" other inmates. Another asked if it was right to intervene if an inmate knew that a homosexual rape was in progress. The discussion program showed that it was possible to create a developmental model which would be effective in modifying both the thinking and the actions of youthful offenders. Analysis of moral judgment pre- and post-tests revealed quite different thinking at the end of the intervention as compared with the beginning. For example, one inmate's pre-test showed a mix between Stage 2 and Stage 3 thinking. In response to the Heinz dilemma, he initially expressed little motivation to steal the drug and little awareness of a Stage 3 moral perspective.

> If he loves her, then he should steal it . . . It depends on the feelings he has for her. He cares for her, so he should steal it if he really cares . . . But its only if he wants to help.

This inmate's post-test (Scored Stage 4/3) indicated a much more mature moral position. By this time he was aware of the moral perspective of the law as well as that of the husband, the wife, and the druggist.

> It's not right to steal, because there is a law against stealing. This here is a situation where it is necessary to steal. The druggist only paid $200 for the drug, and if he gave him a thousand he wouldn't be losing anything. He couldn't lose anything, and his wife's life was on the line. It was necessary to steal the drug to save her life. Still, he broke the law, but the law should still take into consideration that his wife was dying.

Overall, six of the 19 inmates in the experimental group increased in terms of their major stage of moral reasoning (e.g., from Stage 2 to 3, and Stage 3 to 4). Most of the inmates who changed moved from Stage 2 to 3. It was observed that the "changing" inmates were highly involved in the discussions and participated more than did the average member. However, while the program was successful in stimulating development in moral thinking, it was obvious that the discussion groups by themselves could not sustain inmates both within the prison and after release. What was needed was a new, accepting (and controlling) community which would stimulate, welcome, and give social meaning to a "new-life" commitment for the delinquent.

The theory underlying such efforts derives, at least conceptually, from the Durkheimian tradition in sociological theory (18). Durkheim posited that morality is learned through the individual's acceptance of the legitimate norms of a collectivity. Morality is taught through the maintenance of group norms and the rallying of individual identification and support for those norms. Thus, while punishment of an unruly student rarely deters him or others from unruly acts, public punishment serves to articulate, exemplify, and show respect for the rules of the group.

Collective punishment also is critical to the work of Soviet educator and criminologist Anton Makarenko (19) and to "group cohesion" therapies such as those common to the program of Synanon and Daytop. Posed in terms of Kohlberg's theory, it is possible to create a group therapy situation with the cohesiveness and charisma associated with Stage 4 (Synanon-type) groups, but operating according to Stage 5 principles of an open social contract and a pervasive concern with due process and fairness. Thus, while Makarenko sought to resocialize the delinquent into Marxist values, the same means might be used to place him in moral conflict and, through exposure to the perspective of the group and its norms, to generate changes in both thinking and behavior.

This perspective is consistent with Cooley's (20) and Mead's (21) theories of social learning — that an individual's sense of morality derives directly from experiences in group life. For Mead, the learning of conscience emerged from what he calls the "generalized other," or the internalization of the perspective of the group by the individual group member. When a person commits an act which violates the norms of the group, according to Mead, a part of the self views this action as the group might see it. For both Mead and Cooley, an intensive community life is essential to the development within the individual of an adult principled moral perspective.

THE "JUST COMMUNITY" PRISON PROJECT

The focus on creation of a supportive nondelinquent community crystalized into what came to be called a "democratic education" approach to the management of discipline problems in prison. It was hypothesized that, even within the prison context, it might be possible to create the conditions which encourage developmental interaction, create a positive sense of community, and allow for experiences in democratic governance.

Initial efforts to create such an environment were undertaken in 1971 in a Connecticut prison for women. Although mutual hostility between inmates and guards in this institution had almost caused a riot, both inmates and staff expressed some willingness to discuss the possibility of exploring new ways of "co-existing." During the summer months, inmates, guards, and administrators met in what was called a "consituational convention." Negotiations were painful, but the "convention" agreed to experiment with a model cottage and to define limits for a proposed democratic framework. Inmates would control internal discipline, propose furloughs for members, and define program objectives and activities. All prison offenses, with the exception of major felonies, would be referred to a "cottage community meeting."

For the past seven years, decisions have been made through a democratic format created in this convention. A community member can call a meeting at any time. When a cottage-rules offense is discovered, the community meeting acts as jury to determine guilt or innocence. If disciplinary action is in order, it is referred to a discipline board which includes two inmates and one staff member chosen at random. Routine issues involving such matters as work assignments, love triangles, or interpersonal conflicts are dealt with through open dialogue and discussion.

On rare occasions, the "community" deals with issues of contraband, assault, and attempted escape. Cottage rules are redefined every 12 weeks in a "marathon meeting." Here, negotiations with administrators, inmates and staff attempt to define the types of issues over which the cottage democracy will have jurisdiction.

The prison community seeks to establish itself as a new moral referent group. It is hoped that inmates will come to judge their own actions in relation to the moral consensus of the cottage community. Leaders of the group attempt to point out contradictions between an individual's moral statements and his or her actions. (For example, a staff member was reprimanded for "not showing concern in doing her job," while an inmate was punished for not reporting an escape because this showed she "didn't really care about the community".) An excerpt from a "marathon" meeting illustrates the process of prison rule-making. In this meeting, there was a stormy debate about whether or not to require expulsion from the cottage after the first incident involving contraband.

Helen: I feel you got to give a woman a chance.

Tony: I feel if you give a drug-fiend that space she will use it.

Elaine: If I had a chance to use drugs and not get bounced, I would do it.

Gwen: If you have an overly harsh penalty, not all the stuff will come to group. No one will bring a drug thing downstairs knowing someone could get sent out of here.

Tony: You all have never shot dope the way I did. No real dope fiend is gonna bring it up, no matter what.

Pam: Are you saying that, Tony, because you are

going home? What if you had to live here eight or nine more months?

Tony: No, that's not it. Look at Jackie, and what she said (Jackie had just been expelled for drug use): "They allowed me to do it." . . .

Fran: I agree with Tony; if a person comes here looking for help, you gotta be firm.

Judy: I feel they should be allowed one mistake. They should be given one chance; then out.

Tony: You already had your mistake. You are in jail!

Pam: But if they get thrown out of here, they could catch a case in another group, just for weed.

Helen: They don't think about no expulsion or no case. A dope-fiend just acts. She doesn't think.

Ernestine: I don't see it. You can't put a dope-fiend in jail and tell them no dope; it won't work. . .

This excerpt suggests the seriousness and the power of a democratic community, even in prison. When the choice given inmates is an authentic one, a wide range of political opinions tends to be expressed. Some delinquents are more punitive toward one another than even conservative staff members would be. One of the roles played by staff members, therefore, is to temper the judgmental nature of some offenders toward program rule-violators. A staff member may ask the group if the punishment advocated is fair in light of the offense and the offender. A week after the session described above, for example, an unpopular inmate was found in possession of some pills. The group, which had adopted the harsh "one offense and you're out" rule, found itself about to throw this apparent victim of circumstances into the "custody" cottage. A staff member stated in her defense:

I feel really funny throwing Denise out of here. I know she took one or two pills, but I really wonder if you would be as harsh if it was one of the in-crowd?

The group reinstated the woman. Viewing this case objectively, the inmates were forced to reconsider and articulate the meaning of rules, punishment, and fairness. The results of the meeting thus included both a fair decision and a powerful lesson in democratic education.

On balance, the "just community" prison project achievements indicate that it offers both a means of resolving social conflicts in a reasonable manner and a possible effective strategy for political re-education. Nearly one-third of the participants in the model cottage experiment shifted more than half a moral stage (e.g., from Stage 2 to Stage 2/3). These results, which compared favorably with moral education efforts among non-criminal populations, were significantly better than those of both matched untreated controls and treated controls (using intensive moral discussion groups) in traditional prisons.

DEMOCRATIC EDUCATION IN THE SCHOOLS

The concept of the "democratic community" recently has been applied in several projects to determine whether the methods developed in the Connecticut prison project are applicable to public school settings in which many students have had serious confrontations with the law. The first project was initiated by the staff of the Irvine Unified School District and the Program in Social Ecology of the University of California at Irvine. A second project was undertaken by staff of the Cambridge Public Schools and the Center for Moral Education at Harvard University. A third program was established at Brookline High School's "School Within a School" (22).

During the first three years of project operation, some surprisingly similar issues emerged in the three schools. For example, in each school the program established and enforced rules concerning drug use. Students smoking pot in the bathrooms

233

found themselves facing stern juries of their peers. "AWOL," "skips," and "hooks" were similarly addressed as students arrived at appropriate attendance standards and penalties. There has been an effort to turn ordinary school discipline issues into matters of collective concern. A disruptive student, rather then being chastised or sent to the principal, is referred to a discipline committee. Here the matter is either routinely dismissed or referred to the larger community meeting for disposition.

The democratic school represents a major departure from both traditional and "alternative" school programs. While most alternative schools are based on an ideology of individual choice and affective growth, this model assumes that student development occurs most effectively when students participate in democratic decision-making. In addition, while most alternative schools emphasize individual learning contracts and voluntary attendance, these schools have dealt with attendance issues in terms of a democratically derived and maintained school "social contract." The approach differs as well from traditional discipline models by shifting the locus of responsibility for discipline from the teacher to the student-teacher community.

Several problems have emerged in the democratic schools. Classroom discipline at times has conflicted with the rules of the larger school. (In the Brookline project, for example, a student was referred to the community meeting for violating a school rule on political posters. The community meeting promptly acquitted the student, arguing that the school rule was both arbitrary and unnecessary.) The emphasis on group discipline also has tended to take time away from traditional subject areas. A single disciplinary offense may co-opt several hours of the school day. At times also, students have administered disciplines which teachers believed were unfair. (In one democratic school project students punished quite differently two students who had committed identical infractions. The first student, a popular member of the "in" group, received a mild warning. The other student was expelled from school.) Finally, not all students enjoy the type of political involvement demanded by the democratic education approach. Differences in participation may produce a new alienated student group of "non-partici-pators" who come to resent and to withdraw from the school as a whole.

Research in progress by Kohlberg (23) and Scharf (24) indicates that democratic school communities tend to be perceived by students as far more cohesive than traditional school environments. Rules of the democratic school tend to be accepted as legitimate, whereas rules in traditional schools characteristically are perceived as arbitrary and unfair. Teachers report lower rates of school violence and higher rates of school attendance in the democratic school, even among notorious truants. Mutual helpfulness also is observed among students in the democratic school communities. In one school, for example, students went to great pains to reimburse a student who had been robbed by another student. In another, students manned a 24-hours crisis line for students experiencing personal crises. Meetings in these schools are characterized by a common sense of purpose notably absent from most public schools.

Democratic education appears to hold considerable promise for controlling and preventing violence and crime in the public schools. While it is educative, it refrains from "treating" the juvenile who has yet to be convicted of an offense. Further, it both helps to create a school climate in which crime is less likely to occur and serves to teach democratic solutions to social conflicts. An act of violence in the bureaucratic high school is simply a threat to school order and the academic schedule. In the context of the democratic school, it is an opportunity for democratic problem-solving.

FOOTNOTES

1. Erikson, Erik, CHILDHOOD AND SOCIETY (New York, N.Y.: Norton, 1950).
2. Friedlander, Kate, PSYCHOANALYTIC APPROACH TO JUVENILE DELINQUENCY (New York, N.Y.: International Press, 1947).
3. Skinner, B. F., BEYOND FREEDOM AND DIGNITY (New York, N.Y.: Bantam, 1971).
4. Cohen, Albert, DELINQUENT BOYS (Glencoe, Ill.: Free Press, 1955).
5. Yablonski, Lewis, VIOLENT GANG (Baltimore, Md.: Penguin, 1966).
6. Sutherland, Edwin, PRINCIPLES OF CRIMINOLOGY (Philadelphia, Pa.: Lippincott, 1939).
7. Matza, David, DELINQUENCY AND DRIFT (New York, N.Y.: John Wiley, 1968).
8. Parks, Robert and Burgess, Ernest, THE CITY (Chicago, Ill.: University of Chicago Press, 1925).
9. Miller, Walter, "Lower Class Culture as a Generating Milieu of Gang Delinquency," JOURNAL OF SOCIAL ISSUES, 14(5): 1958.
10. Merton, Robert, SOCIAL STRUCTURE AND SOCIAL THEORY (Glencoe, Ill.: Free Press, 1956).
11. Cloward, Richard and Ohlin, Lloyd, DELINQUENCY AND OPPORTUNITY (New York, N.Y.: Free Press, 1960).
12. Empey, Lamar, THE SILVERLAKE EXPERIMENT (Chicago, Ill: Aldine, 1971).
13. Kohlberg, Lawrence, "Moral development: A Review of Theory," THEORY INTO PRACTICE, 16(2): 1977.
14. Kohlberg, Lawrence and Freundlich, "Moral Reasoning Among Delinquent Youth," Unpublished paper, Harvard University 1972.
15. Kohlberg, Lawrence and Mosher, Ralph, Unpublished report to the Ford Foundation, 1976.
16. Blatt, Moshe, "Moral Discussion with Adolescents," JOURNAL OF MORAL EDUCATION, 12 (2): 1975.

17. Fenton, Edwin, "Moral Education: Research Findings" in Scharf (ed.), READINGS IN MORAL EDUCATION (Minneapolis, Minn.: Winston Press, 1978).

18. Durkheim, Emile, MORAL EDUCATION (Glencoe, Ill.: Free Press, 1960).

19. Makarenko, Anton, ROAD TO LIFE (Moscow: Foreign Languages Press, 1955).

20. Cooley, Charles, SOCIAL ORGANIZATION (New York, N.Y.: Schocken, 1926).

21. Mead, George H., MIND, SELF, SOCIETY (Chicago, Ill.: University of Chicago Press, 1937).

22. Scharf, Peter, "School Democracy: Promise and Paradox," in Scharf (ed.), READINGS IN MORAL EDUCATION (Minneapolis, Minn: Winston Press, 1978).

23. Kohlberg, Lawrence, "Foreword," Scharf (ed.), READINGS IN MORAL EDUCATION (Minneapolis, Minn.: Winston Press, 1978).

24. Scharf, Peter, "A Developmental Psychologist's View of Alternative Education" in Felton (ed.), VALUES, CONCEPTS, AND STRATEGIES (Washington, D.C.: National Education Association, 1976).

DIALOGUE BOOKS®

A persistent and frustrating problem for both the human service professional and the social action advocate is the fragmentation of information on important social topics. Most social science information is scattered throughout a vast publication system, a fact which seriously obstructs the development of effective approaches to social problems.

RESPONSIBLE ACTION brings together a wide range of opinion and information on timely and important topics in its DIALOGUE BOOKS series. DIALOGUE BOOKS are written for people in education and the human services, or others who care about social progress generally; but they also depend on the interest and support of this varied readership. A dynamic interchange – an ongoing dialogue – with people who work within the many disciplines in this field is essential if these publications are to remain current, relevant, and based on practical experience.RESPONSIBLE ACTION attempts through its ASSOCIATE PROGRAM to form the foundation for such a productive dialogue.

1978 DIALOGUE BOOKS

STRESS, DISTRESS, AND GROWTH
MORAL EDUCATION
PARTNERSHIP IN RESEARCH
THE VALUE OF YOUTH
DELINQUENCY PREVENTION: Educational Approaches
SCHOOL CRIME AND DISRUPTION: Prevention Models
DROPOUT
THE YOUNG ADULT OFFENDER

DIALOGUE BOOKS are quality paperback editions.
Price: $ 5.75   Student Manuals and Workbooks $ 3.75

Order your books through your local bookstore or through RESPONSIBLE ACTION.

RESPONSIBLE ACTION, P.O.Box 924, Davis, California 95616